"*Good Night, Lord* i[s]
ryone can enjoy e
will touch your h[e]
who are exhausted
to rest in tranquility. In the quiet moments before retiring, this book invites you to experience intimate conversation with the God who surrounds you with
boundless love—no matter what kind of day you've
had. It is a perfect way to end the day. Insightful, inspiring, and stimulating!"

Bridget Mary Meehan
Author, *Prayers, Activities and Celebrations*
for Catholic Families

"Fr. Joseph Sullivan has a prayerful heart. His entire life
has been focused on prayer and the art of writing his
deepest sentiments before the Lord. His new book, *Good
Night, Lord: Everyday Prayers for Everyday People*, is the
fruit of his deep holiness. A blend of thoughtful re-
flections and heartfelt yearnings—it fills the soul with
delight. It brings one closer to Almighty God. You'll find
these daily meditations filled with grace and beauty."

Rev. John Catoir
Director, The Christophers

"I found that *Good Night, Lord* triggered a wide range of
emotions in me. Taken as a body, the prayers called me
to reflect and remember God's place in my life and in all
that I do. Father Sullivan's prayers, whether read in silence or spoken aloud, should help us end each day with
gratitude for the gifts and challenges that God has given
us."

Charles J. Schisla
Director, Public Policy Information
Archdiocese of Indianapolis

GOOD NIGHT,
LORD

Everyday Prayers for Everyday People

JOSEPH T. SULLIVAN

TWENTY-THIRD PUBLICATIONS
Mystic, Connecticut 06355

Nihil obstat
Michel J. St. Pierre
Censor Librorum

Imprimatur
Most Reverend Kenneth A. Angell
Bishop of Burlington
June 23, 1995

Twenty-Third Publications
185 Willow Street
P.O. Box 180
Mystic, CT 06355
(860) 536-2611
800-321-0411

ISBN 0-89622-681-6
Library of Congress Catalog Card Number 95-61810
Printed in the U.S.A.

Contents

Invitation

How accessible is God? Always present, God is only a prayer away.

Good Night, Lord provides prayers for everyone, one for each day of the year. They speak to God in everyday language, expressing the concerns, hopes, disappointments, sorrows, needs, joys of everyday people like you.

Your relationship with God develops through dialogue, through listening. In prayer you converse with the most lovable and most loving God. In prayer you are in contact with Someone who loves you individually, personally, with an overwhelming love.

Should a prayer especially appeal to you, pray it often, regardless of the day; reflect on it, line by line, savoring it. If another should not appeal to you, pass it over and let your heart speak—or listen—spontaneously to God. In either event, pray daily and pray often.

May these prayers be, for you, the occasion for more prolonged prayer.

GOOD NIGHT, LORD

Mistakes

I made some mistakes today, Lord.
So, what else is new?
They happen to everyone—to err is human, they say.
But now I'm wiser.
Errors keep me humble,
    prevent me from going into orbit with a swelled head.
Mistakes can bring me closer to others, if I'm honest.
Laughing at them isn't a bad idea, either;
    others laugh with me and we relate to one another.
Looking back over my waking hours, I pray
    that you will forgive me for all my faults.
You always do—when I'm sorry for them.
I am encouraged and at peace as this day closes.
Good night, Lord.

Happy People

Lord, I meet happy people and ask myself
    why I'm not a happier person.
Most of the time I don't think about
    whether I'm happy or not.
If someone ever asks me, I have to stop and think.
This happiness thing is so relative.
Some people appear cheerful despite difficulties;
    others moan and groan all the day long.
This has been a typical day.
Having faith in you is a big factor
    in this elusive pursuit of happiness.
I know that life can be happy if you are with me.
You are the source of all goodness, happiness itself.
Good night, Lord.

January 3
Wonderful World
Lord, every day we see little children—
   beautiful, so trusting and affectionate.
Seeing them really moves me;
   we want to introduce them to a wonder-full world.
As we grow older, we take things for granted;
   not so the children!
They are in an age of discovery and adventure.
It would be great to recapture my childhood curiosity.
As this day dwindles,
   bless me with a childlike purity of spirit.
I look forward to tomorrow
   when there is so much more to be discovered.
Thanks for the graces of this day.
Good night, Lord.

January 4
No Hopeless Cases
Lord, for a while, I thought I was cornered,
   in an impossible situation.
At the end of the day now, I see things differently,
   you know, with a different perspective.
I understand why they say your ways are mysterious.
In the light of your providential care,
   there are no hopeless cases.
I need to reflect on your goodness in difficult times.
Help everyone who feels pressured as I did today.
All of us need to look up and live,
   to trust that in your love you are with me.
Give me your peace.
I place myself in your hands.
Good night, Lord.

Relishing the Moment

Lord, thinking back on today's events,
    I wish I had savored every moment.
Nothing particularly great happened;
    it's just that I take each day for granted
    as if the day and all that happens were due to me.
I know I've said this before:
    if I could live it over, I'd try to relish each day more.
I forget your loving presence.
Each moment is to be lived
    as one blessing follows another.
Goodness and beauty surround me.
Thanks for wonderful moments I did appreciate.
I look forward to a wonderful tomorrow.
Good night, Lord.

Friendship

I met a friend today, Lord,
    and remembered that friendship is precious.
Friends are on our wavelength.
They talk, laugh, and share with ease.
They are in concert with our ideas and feelings.
They are at our celebrations,
    and with us in times of distress.
Friends understand their friends.
You, Lord, are my unchanging friend.
Ours is not a business relationship,
    or one between master and slave.
You are my God and my special friend.
For all my friends, especially you, thank you.
Good night, Lord.

January 7
Difficult Moments

The day is done, Lord;
  I survived the difficult moments.
I never know when I get up
  what is in store for me.
Praise to you, Lord, for the good times—
  and the bad.
We are in a lasting relationship, you and I;
  you sustain me, care for me.
I really ought to express my gratitude to you
  for unpleasant situations, for times of challenge.
Still, if I'm to be consistent, it does make sense.
You are always present, perhaps especially present
  when the going gets rough.
Good night, Lord.

January 8
War Victims

As I lie down to sleep, Lord, I reflect on war
  and the thought leaves me restless.
The news reports violence and conflict the world over.
Thousands of refugees flee across borders;
  once secure in their homes, now they are homeless,
  driven from one forsaken place to another.
Hospitals overflow with the wounded,
  all emotionally and psychologically scarred.
Sensitize my heart to the sufferings
  of all my brothers and sisters, on both sides.
Let me never become accustomed and callous
  to their desperate plight.
Grant us peace, the world over.
Good night, Lord.

Equal Rights

It's strange, Lord, how our minds float back at bedtime
    to the day's controversies and debates:
    affirmative action, welfare reform, gun control,
    abortion, budget slashing, and children's welfare.
There is so much protest, despair, banner-carrying—
    and anger.
Whatever the issue is, inspire us with the vision
    to see one another as you created us,
    as brothers and sisters in your one family.
Free our minds from prejudice and selfishness.
Give us the grace to really love one another.
Let me have a peaceful night's sleep,
    resolved to be generous tomorrow.
Good night, Lord.

Ideal Girl

Rummaging through some collectibles, Lord,
    I rediscovered a poem, "The Ideal Girl."
It speaks of someone gentle, kind, and sweet.
It says nothing about body measurements,
    hair color, or designer labels.
Somewhere in scripture, there's a line suggesting
    the beauty of the king's daughter is from within.
Cosmetics and style do not figure as prominently
    as character, positive outlook, and moral goodness.
May I learn over a lifetime
    to see what is important in others and in myself.
    and may I learn as well not to judge others.
As the day winds down, bless me with a true perspective.
Good night, Lord.

January 11
Being Afraid

There were a few anxious moments today, Lord.
Sometimes, I am fearful;
    it comes without any warning.
Life's circumstances seem to slip out of alignment.
I see other people full of confidence,
    moving with poise and equanimity.
Do you allow trying moments to keep me humble?
Are these moments to prevent me from becoming
    too independent and self-reliant?
My anxiety disappears with renewed trust in you.
Thanks for these beneficial trials.
I should not forget your tremendous love for me.
Let me fall asleep and then waken with that thought.
Good night, Lord.

January 12
Humor

It was a good day, Lord.
It started with a joke.
Someone told me a funny story,
    (but now I can't remember it).
People with a sunny disposition are fun,
    especially those who can turn words for a laugh.
We need more comedians to brighten up our lives,
    ordinary folk with a good sense of humor.
It's not good to be stricken with seriousness.
Comical friends who do not offend us
    or disparage others brighten our lives.
Thanks for all those who lighten our days.
They help us see that life is worth living.
Good night, Lord.

Undergoing Surgery

I visited the hospital recently, Lord.
It really made an impression on me.
People are prepared for surgery—a major challenge
    as they submit to tests, X-rays, and blood samples.
Medical teams of doctors, nurses, and technicians
    coordinate their efforts.
Give them skills and compassion, Lord.
Calm the patients about to enter operating theaters.
(I may be in their place some day!)
Settle their minds and hearts
    with ideal submission to your holy will.
Help me to appreciate life and not lose sight
    of your love, no matter what the challenge.
Good night, Lord.

Tact

Lord, thinking back over the day—
    examining my conscience—
    I wonder about my thoughtless words.
It seems I have to guard against flippancy,
    putting my foot in my mouth
    while trying to be clever.
I do try to be sensitive.
It's possible to kid some folks good-naturedly,
    others, not at all.
Honestly, I've got to work at discretion and tact.
My tongue, being in a wet place, is apt to slip.
I hope I haven't offended anyone.
If I have, unwittingly, I place them in your hands.
Good night, Lord.

January 15
Immeasurable Love

It's a mathematical world, Lord:
    60 seconds in a minute, 60 minutes an hour,
    168 hours in a week.
In this age of the computer, we can calculate
    zillions of digits in a flash.
We figure out orbits of rockets,
    whizzing through space to the moon and Mars.
You have endowed us with the ability
    to measure motion with uncanny accuracy,
    no matter how great the distance.
Your love for me, however, is something else;
    that is truly immeasurable!
How comforting to know you are only a prayer away.
Good night, Lord.

January 16
Forgiveness

In the quiet moments before retiring, Lord,
    I am in a forgiving mood.
This is not condescension.
It's realistic that somebody—sometime—
    is going to hurt me, offend me.
It's senseless to respond with undue anger
    or worse, with some form of violence.
This only escalates in a vicious cycle.
How often I have asked to be forgiven
    as I forgive others for their offenses.
Bearing wrongs patiently is what I wish from others.
Forgiving is loving,
    and I know you love me.
Good night, Lord.

Against the Grain

I had a resolution at the start of this day:
    to pray for someone I dislike, Lord.
Anyone can love those who love them.
There is a mutuality, a reciprocity in that.
Love generates love—
    even the godless can do that.
But to try honestly to love my enemies, my critics,
    those who bug me—
    that's being magnanimous.
I like to think I have that kind of character.
Loving my "enemies" goes against the grain,
    but that is a big part of holiness, isn't it?
I hope you are pleased with my resolution.
Good night, Lord.

Parental Discretion

I noticed a sign today, Lord,
    that read, "Parental Discretion Advised."
It is attached to so many movies and TV shows.
Parents, it says, think twice about this film;
    it may endanger your children!
Judging from the multiplication of warnings,
    there are dangers all over the place.
Mothers and fathers need your help, Lord.
There are so many influences in society
    that may harm their children in some way.
Bless families everywhere; inspire them to pray together.
They need your guidance and grace.
Send your Spirit to guide us all.
Good night, Lord.

January 19

Teachers

Driving by a school earlier today, Lord,
   I thought about my old teachers.
Most of us can name some of those
   who influenced us years ago in grade school.
Bless all the good men and women
   to whom we entrust our children.
Inspire them with the most noble intentions.
Endow them with true human values.
May they be believers, citizens of faith in you, Lord.
Reward them for their patience and understanding,
   their good efforts and sacrifices.
Let them always lead our children closer to you.
I pray for a sound sleep.
Good night, Lord.

January 20

Quiet Prayer

This is the most peaceful part of the day, Lord.
Speak to my heart.
I am quiet and still and receptive.
The day's duties and details are done,
   and I am not in a hurry or anxious.
My room for the moment is a chapel
   and I invite you in for a visit.
Dispensing with every distraction,
   I pray I might be open to your words.
"Speak, Lord, for your servant is listening."
I don't expect voices or apparitions,
   just your comfort and guidance.
Be with me this night and always.
Good night, Lord.

Monotony

This has been a routine day, Lord—
    not that I do not appreciate it as a gift.
Despite talent and creative ability,
    boring repetition is inescapable.
Zillions of dishes are washed, socks laundered,
    gas tanks filled, papers corrected, shoes shined.
Realistically, I can't expect adventure every hour.
There are so many things I do over and over.
Thanks for the grace of patience.
Let me see the value and purpose of it all.
I offer you all my days,
    even though—and especially when—
    they are monotonous and uneventful.
Good night, Lord.

Rejoicing

I rejoiced in success today, Lord,
    another's, not mine.
Sharing someone's joy is a blessing in itself.
Life is so much more fulfilling
    when a child discovers pretty butterflies,
    or a student proudly shows me a term paper.
I can sense how my enthusiasm and excitement
    buoy their human spirit.
Happy moments are precious, highlights of living.
Everyone needs approval, especially yours, Lord.
Let me continue to celebrate your blessings
    and join in the celebrations of others.
It's been a good day.
Good night, Lord.

Smiling

Lord, I'm thinking about my morning offering,
    my resolution to smile more,
      to smile when I don't feel like it.
Smiling is an icebreaker;
    it tempers the impatient and the angered;
    it dissolves hostility.
People who smile brighten the world
    and lighten the burdens that others carry.
I can't say I've developed a habit of it.
It really calls for a big-hearted person.
I remember the sign,
    "Keep Smiling! God loves you!"
Your love is enough to make anyone smile.
Good night, Lord.

Trust

How can I get through a day without trust?
I'm glad to renew my confidence in you, Lord.
Tomorrow, when I wake,
    there will still be problems from today.
If I solved them all right away,
    there wouldn't be anything to do.
Just kidding!
Still, where are last week's worries?
Some have gone, faded from memory.
With you, there are no problems I cannot conquer,
    or at least face them with courage and resolve.
This thought gives me comfort
    as I rest my weary head on the pillow.
Good night, Lord.

Perseverance

I made it through the day, Lord.
It wasn't bad—the usual challenges.
Some time ago, third graders made me a sign:
    "Keep Me Going, Lord!"
Were they trying to tell me something?
It's universally applicable and one size fits all.
My eye catches the sign now and then.
It helps me when I'm going at top speed
    and frustration brings me to a standstill.
The children would laugh if they knew
    how much their sign helps.
Of course, I know it is you, Lord,
    who is the real source of my strength.
Good night, Lord.

Driving

I found myself grinding my teeth
    while driving through traffic.
It's those other drivers, Lord. Really.
My personality splits when I'm driving.
Somebody said of me:
    this normally considerate guy loses it
    when weaving among slow-moving vehicles.
I have to tell myself
    that they have just as much right on the road.
Now, at the end of this trying day,
    I realize we are all members of the same family,
    and I should treat them
    as I'd like them to treat me.
Good night, Lord.

Creation

Lord, we are all on a continual spin
    as this blue marble we call Planet Earth
    turns delicately and precisely on its axis.
Morning to night to morning,
    century after endless century.
We circle the sun, spinning like a top,
    as our moon circles us.
We understand so much more today
    than when people thought Earth was flat,
    even more than just a decade ago.
Since dawn this morning, I have been conscious
    of your marvelous creation.
May my appreciation of it increase.
Good night, Lord.

Gratitude

Showing appreciation, Lord, is indispensable.
I sometimes reflect on my many blessings
    and how kind people have been.
Have I said thanks often enough?
From the bottom of my heart?
Ten lepers were cured miraculously
    but only one returned to give thanks.
Is this typical of me?
You, Lord, are the giver of all gifts.
Everything I have—everything—comes from you.
Pardon my ingratitude.
Thank you for life and all its graces.
I appreciate your love and generosity.
Good night, Lord.

Resourcefulness

"Where there's a will, there's a way."
An old expression, but valid despite its age.
"Can do" people think this way.
You, Lord, equip us with great resourcefulness.
I marvel at the adaptation of plants and animals.
Even more am I impressed with human abilities.
Created after your image and likeness,
    we are endowed with remarkable ingenuity.
Reviewing the day's variety of challenges,
    I know most problems can be solved
    or intelligently approached.
Endow me with this gift of resourcefulness,
    and may I use it to do your will.
Good night, Lord.

Uptight

Things go better with a laugh or two, Lord.
Taking life too seriously is a hindrance in itself.
I'm not thinking of irresponsibility or a cop-out.
Still, being too uptight all the time
    does not make me a better disciple.
The athlete of God has to be loose.
Folks have to remind me now and then to relax.
I forget I am constantly in your loving presence.
This should give me a certain confidence
    and ease, knowing you are at my side.
Grant me tonight the desire to work hard,
    the wisdom to know my limitations,
    and a penetrating sense of your presence.
Good night, Lord.

Considerateness

Considerateness was my objective today, Lord.
It's more than a new word;
 I want to make it a goal for every day.
Considerateness works wonders everywhere.
It means tolerance for others' tastes,
 preferences, and points of view.
Considerateness plays stereos softly
 and takes people's feelings into account.
It reminds me of the ancient expression,
 "A soft answer turns away wrath."
Considerateness radiates love and respect.
I'm sorry for my failures today;
 I'll try harder tomorrow to be considerate.
Good night, Lord.

No Complaints

This morning, Lord, I gave myself
    the goal of being completely positive.
"No complaints today," I promised myself.
I never realized how challenging it would be.
No negatives about the coffee or food,
    about other drivers, or the store clerk.
Bashing the government or politicians was out;
    bad-mouthing the clergy, too.
The weather was ideal.
The dogs didn't bark and the flies disappeared.
Do you think my friends suspected
    something was wrong with me?
There is so much to thank you for.
Good night, Lord.

Prisoners

Prisoners have been on my mind, Lord.
I imagine myself in their shoes.
How trying and painful can life get?
It's difficult to lose freedom.
Guilty or innocent, repentant or defiant,
    they are confined, restricted.
They all need encouragement:
    prisoners of war, criminals in county prisons.
They all need hope.
They will receive justice and mercy from you, Lord.
Free all of us, Lord, from the shackles of sin.
There isn't anyone who doesn't need a second chance.
Inspire us to treat all prisoners humanely.
Good night, Lord.

February 3
Home Harmony
There is no place like home.
We want it to be a special place, Lord,
    a sanctuary, a haven of peace.
Of course, it isn't always like that.
Behind the front door lie challenges, problems.
Harmony and forgiveness don't just happen;
    they must be cultivated.
Kindness is to be spoken within these walls.
There has to be give and take—
    expressions like "I'm sorry," and "I love you."
Be present in this home, Lord,
    and fill it with your love.
May we be mindful of your loving presence.
Good night, Lord.

February 4
Medical Professionals
"If you are in distress,
    we'll sew a tear in your happiness"
    —a line from an old radio ad for a tailor.
Many people, Lord, try hard to mend the pain
    in people whose lives have been torn apart,
    medical pros who devote their lives
    to alleviating suffering and disability.
Bless them and bring out the best in them.
Strengthen them, Lord, when they grow weary;
    buoy them up when their spirits flag.
Comfort those who are ill
    and those who care for them.
Your grace is sufficient for them all.
Good night, Lord.

Distractions

Lord, my thoughts are here and there,
    like butterflies going from blossom to blossom.
How I can flit from topic to topic.
In my daydreams, I travel far and near.
Bless me, Lord, with focus and concentration
    at work, conversing, praying, care-giving;
    it demands all the discipline I can muster.
Students, scientists, pilots, musicians—
    all have to overcome distractions.
Of course, distractions are welcome to relax us.
    a change in scenery, for the human spirit.
Life can be a flood of distractions, Lord,
    but may I never lose sight of you.
Good night, Lord.

Delight in the Lord

As this day darkens, Lord,
    so many of its details float past in memory.
What should stand out is how delighted
    I ought to be in just knowing you,
    in just having you share this day.
The psalmist says, "Take delight in the Lord."
When I see old friends or relatives,
    my hearts often skips with delight.
Mindful of your tremendous love,
    how much more should I delight in you.
And how much delight you take in me
    and in all my brothers and sisters.
May we all approach you confidently.
Good night, Lord.

Goals

Lord, life becomes more interesting
    when there are goals to strive for.
Goals channel our efforts, give meaning
    and purpose to our waking hours.
St. Paul tells us to "direct our thoughts
    to all that is true, all that deserves respect,
    all that is honest, pure, admirable, decent,
    virtuous or worthy of praise."
He's talking real holiness for daily living.
I know I shouldn't stumble around aimlessly, Lord.
Life is more than pursuing pleasure;
    my life finds its destiny in you.
How oriented have I been today?
Good night, Lord.

Honorable Conduct

Many read the Bible to jump-start their day.
Lord, I know you are pleased with that
    and that I should read your holy book
    much more often than I do.
It is your word to me this day and every day.
How timeless the word you offer,
    applicable from morning to night, in every age.
You tell us through Paul's pen that our conduct
    is to be honorable in the eyes of all.
Whatever I do, wherever I go,
    it is up to me—by your grace—
    to be honorable, genuine, and true.
I pray that I may know your word better.
Good night, Lord.

Self-Esteem

Lord, hardly a day goes by without
    someone talking about self-esteem.
It seems it was always this way,
    focusing on how high or low we rate ourselves.
Paul had to tell the Romans
    not to be wise in their own estimation.
It is far better to be humble,
    (which is a way of saying realistic, honest)
    than to give myself credit
    for what is really due to another.
Let my esteem of myself be balanced and fair.
If I feel inadequate or under-appreciated,
    I know that at least I am precious to you.
Good night, Lord.

Knowing God

"Getting to know you," Lord, is a line from a song.
 A day doesn't go by without the opportunity
    of coming to know you better, Lord.
We discover your goodness everywhere:
    in fleecy clouds, in flowers, in fragrant blossoms,
    in a crowded mall, and in a keg of nails.
"The heavens and Earth are the work of your hands."
If we see with comprehension and understanding,
    the evidence surrounds us, even overwhelms us.
If we can read the signs, we can get to know you.
We may not fathom all the wonders of Earth,
    but we can learn more about you, our Creator.
Thanks for all your blessings.
Good night, Lord.

February 11

Humor

Lord, I am weary at the end of this day.
Humor and laughter on a day like this
    proved a great spirit-builder, an elixir;
    cheerful people and amusing stories
    were medicine for my spent soul.
The world, like a gigantic pressure pot,
    is moderated with a joke or two.
Thanks, Lord, for those who added humor
    to the day's grind and dark moments.
Laughter softened and brightened the day.
Help me to laugh to myself, Lord,
    to relax, manage tomorrow's challenges,
    and praise you with an unburdened heart.
Good night, Lord.

February 12

Nature and God

The shades of night are falling.
I cannot see you, Lord, but I know you are here.
Signs of you are all around me.
How could the complicated marvel of the human body
    come into existence without your artistry?
Creation, the work of your hands,
    reveals who you are, what you are like:
    whitecaps on the lake, gray skies cloaking the sun,
    leaves trembling in the wind—
    all testify to your loving presence.
Help me, Lord, to know you, to read the signs,
    to find you in what you have made.
Let me fall asleep reassured that you are near.
Good night, Lord.

Correction

Correction is a good thing, Lord.
If students' tests are not corrected,
 they go on making the same mistakes.
Sinners—all of us—are people
 who harm others, are unloving.
Correction, an admonition, gentle and firm,
 is in order.
In kindness, we must be concerned for one another.
Bless me, Lord, with the gentle grace of tact.
I must be encouraging and compassionate,
 not condescending, judgmental, or superior.
As I close my eyes for this day,
 inspire me to guide my friends toward you.
Good night, Lord.

Questions

A day doesn't go by, Lord, without questions.
We ask directions, seek counsel, wonder why.
Children drive parents bananas asking questions.
There are the big questions, too—
 about life, about destiny, life after death.
Everyone searches, peering into microscopes,
 lifting stones, paging through books,
 talking to experts, scrolling computers.
We all want answers, so we keep on looking.
I saw a sign years ago that read,
 "The Answer Is God!"
I really can't quarrel with that.
Thanks for my faith and your guidance.
Good night, Lord.

Marvelous Self

Lord, how marvelously you have created us.
We are mysterious even to ourselves.
People can multiply large numbers rapidly,
    without calculators or computers.
Others communicate eloquently without scripts.
Some precisely predict the trajectory of comets.
Still others endure hardship to explore strange lands.
How is it that the arteries, muscles, and bones
    work so efficiently?
How explain the tie between thought and emotion?
Whatever we are capable of, Lord,
    we have you to thank.
Make me ever truly grateful.
Good night, Lord.

February 16
Forgiveness

If we expect forgiveness, Lord, we must forgive.
Victims and their families sometimes scream
    at perpetrators judged guilty in court.
They have been wrongfully harmed by criminals.
    and deserve our sympathy and support.
But to be released from bitterness,
    they must let go of anger and vengeance.
"It is in pardoning that we are pardoned."
It is a difficult lesson, a paradoxical one,
    something seemingly impossible yet true.
Forgive us our trespasses, Lord,
    as we forgive those who trespass against us.
There is no other way but your loving way.
Good night, Lord.

Happiness

I've spent most of this day, Lord,
pursuing happiness, haven't I?
Where is it to be found?
In big money games, adventure,
dollars, and endless possessions?
We look for it in approval and praise.
We search for the perfect spouse to join hearts
in a lifelong, loving relationship.
Our souls are restless.
We fly from flower to flower for the nectar of delight.
The Sermon on the Mount suggests other directions:
purity of heart, mercy, peacemaking, simplicity.
Only you are the source of all goodness and blessing.
Good night, Lord.

Lived Convictions

Lord, strengthen me in my convictions.
There are times when I must take a stand
for my belief in you, when I must have
the courage of my convictions.
Not everyone who says "Lord, Lord"
will enter the kingdom of heaven.
Fulfilling your holy will, Lord,
is the chief conviction of my life.
Not my will, but your will be done.
Eternal life, paradise, is not automatic;
it calls for decision, for follow-through.
Tomorrow let me show, as opportunities arise,
that you are my first conviction.
Good night, Lord.

February 19

Noble Things

"The noble person does noble things."
By your grace, Lord, may I live nobly.
It is another way of saying my status as your child
    demands that I live lovingly.
It is an old message, ever new.
Deceiving a person is not high-minded or noble.
Exploiting the weak, taking advantage of the poor
    is clearly ignoble.
Being clever at another's expense is not clever at all.
Living extravagantly—conspicuous consumption—
    is not noble living.
Every day there are temptations, Lord.
Help me to act with true nobility.
Good night, Lord.

February 20

Inner Peace

Bless me with inner peace, Lord.
Help me not to nurse anger inside.
A calm exterior sometimes belies
    the fire burning within.
With a smoldering interior,
    there is always danger of an explosion.
It is wise to coordinate my inside and outside,
    becoming thoroughly whole, genuinely tranquil.
If I have a good reason to be angry and upset,
    I can still have inner peace.
Help me to realize that this is a peace
    that no one can take from me.
Give me the flexibility to roll with life's punches.
Good night, Lord.

Abiding Hope

Nothing is really hopeless, Lord,
    because you are with me.
If I am in your good graces, all is well.
Of that I am certain.
Despite troubles and temptations,
    your strength is sufficient for me.
Teach me to discern what can be changed
    and to endure what must be endured.
Grant me courage and inspiration.
Lift my spirits and calm my anxieties.
Life is short and distractions many.
May I never take my eyes from the goal:
    union, happiness with you.
Good night, Lord.

Openness

A spirit of openness is a great blessing.
Reflecting on this day and on the past
    makes that perfectly clear, Lord.
Everyone hears according to their disposition.
The reception is flavored.
Our own thoughts color the message
    and prejudgments temper it.
One homily in church may be received
    in as many ways as there are listeners.
Enable me, Lord, to be open to the truth
    wherever I may find it,
    however disagreeable it may be.
Help me to embrace your word honestly.
Good night, Lord.

February 23

Confidence

"I can do it, Lord; it's really do-able."
Thinking like this reflects my confidence.
There is power in positive thinking.
A spirit-filled, undersized team
    can scrap its way to the championship.
Underlying the confidence needed in life's
    challenges is a genuine trust in you.
If you are with me, Lord,
    who can prevail over me?
There is nothing we can't handle together.
I have to work diligently, Lord,
    as if it all depends on me,
    and pray humbly as if all depends on you.
Good night, Lord.

February 24

Planning

There's a story, Lord, about Grandma
    fingering through her prayer books,
    as if, her grandchildren say,
    she is cramming for her finals.
All of us are pilgrims on a journey,
    which, long or short, will lead us to you.
If fuel is stored for the winter
    and money put aside for emergencies,
    then following your will is my preparation
    for my most important encounter.
Grant that I may prepare wisely, day by day,
    so that, at journey's end,
    and by your grace, I may meet you.
Good night, Lord.

Opportunity

Each day is an opportunity.
How can I praise you tomorrow, Lord,
    honor you and give you glory?
In countless ways, by whatever challenges me:
    unforgiving friends and family death,
    financial crisis and serious illness,
    or flat tires and mistakes at work.
I can greet every challenge with a smile—
    or at least with a determined heart.
When I am tried, I can prove
    myself true—with your grace.
You call me, Lord, not so much to be successful
    as to be faithful.
Good night, Lord.

Better Ways

There are better ways, Lord.
Every day we observe human potential.
Creativity and imagination have no limit;
    you have created us resourceful.
Successful inventions show us that:
    in communicating, building, traveling,
    and even in cooking.
They provide promise for a better tomorrow.
It is very encouraging and the future is bright.
If only, Lord, we used the same resourcefulness
    to give you honor and glory.
Make us conscious that all gifts
    are to be used for the good of all people.
Good night, Lord.

February 27

Limitations

It is wise to recognize my limitations, Lord.
I have great potential, but I remain
  absolutely dependent on you.
There is only one truly independent being,
  and it is you.
There is nothing belittling about that.
No one can do it all.
There are no specialists in all fields;
  this keeps me humble.
I am encouraged to be strong in faith,
  and faithful enough to move mountains.
This faith rests in you, who are almighty.
How reassuring to know you are all-loving, too.
Good night, Lord.

February 28

Gratitude

In our conversations, Lord,
  I should pray with more appreciation.
You listen.
You respond.
You care and you love.
You are not distant or disinterested
  but close and responsive,
  closer than I can imagine.
Everything I have comes from you,
  my most generous benefactor.
Singularly blessed, I see you as my loving parent,
  the giver of all good gifts.
Thank you for all that you are.
Good night, Lord.

Constant Love

You are very pleased, Lord,
    when we love one another.
No one is to be excluded
    from our kindness and compassion.
It is not really an option.
Our love for one another should be constant,
    as St. Peter wrote.
It is good to know I can atone for my sins
    by my care and concern for others.
Let my love, Lord, be like a warm flame,
    never dimming, but steady and dependable.
I sleep now, knowing that
    your love for me never dies.
Good night, Lord.

March 1
Scheduling God In
I live in a fast-moving world, Lord.
Many of us hit the road running,
    taking care of demands from dawn to dusk.
Some have pocket planners to keep track
    of appointments and responsibilities.
What we really need, Lord,
    are reminders that include you
    in our day-to-day affairs.
In our busy, preoccupied culture
    we need to redirect our thoughts to you
    so that we don't lose our way.
Help me to seek first your kingdom,
    to make that my priority.
Good night, Lord.

March 2
Praise God
Everything gives you glory, Lord.
Rock-creviced wildflowers praise you,
    as does a quiet walk through a forest
    where the hemlocks stand in reverence.
And notes of jazz down an unlistening street.
Leaf-cutter ants also praise you,
    and so do the mountain ranges of Nepal
    and the plains of Africa with innumerable herds.
Deep canyons and pounding surf
    a half-moon and the Milky Way praise you.
All this is your handiwork, Lord.
We recognize the touch of your creative hands;
    your world tells us what you are like.
Good night, Lord.

Better Person

Make me a better person, Lord.
It's a simple prayer, I know,
    but you won't re-create me to start anew.
Being better has to come from within me—
    now, as I am this very night.
They say such a reform is like sowing seeds.
If I sow an act, I reap a habit;
    if I sow a habit, I reap a character;
    if I sow a character, I reap a destiny.
Becoming better means often going against the grain.
It has to do with loving, which is kind, patient . . .
Let me put today aside and begin tomorrow
    with small acts of love for others.
Good night, Lord.

Public Servants

Public servants deserve our prayers, Lord.
Presidents, governors, mayors—
    all are servants of the people.
They are often suspected of ulterior motives,
    hidden agendas, feathering their own nests,
    but many are dedicated and humble.
Give them wisdom and courage, Lord,
    to seek and work for the common good,
    to be concerned about the least in our society.
Endow them with good judgment and honesty
    based on your holy will.
May we all be supportive, assisting one another
    for the benefit of all.
Good night, Lord.

March 5
Meeting Challenges
Lord, there's a solution to every problem.
They say when we come to the end of our rope,
    to tie a knot and hang on.
It's important not to feel sorry for ourselves,
    but to work toward a solution,
      even if it is painful at the time.
Life is full of injustices and we all have a share.
Generous people bear wrongs patiently,
    but they work to set things right.
I tend to blow up misfortunes
    when they are my own.
Give me the grace to rise to every occasion,
    to meet every challenge gracefully.
Good night, Lord.

March 6
Writers
There is so much print around these days, Lord.
Somebody has to do this writing,
    but very few writers are acclaimed.
Working with words is their stock in trade.
Often we think of words flowing creatively,
    even effortlessly from their genius,
      but writing must be difficult and painful at times,
      especially if they write responsibly.
Authors, word wizards, know it is demanding.
Bless, Lord, all those who write: reporters and poets,
    novelists and scientists, playwrights and analysts.
Inspire them to be truthful, never using their talents
    merely for notoriety or financial gain.
Good night, Lord.

The Poor

Millions of my brothers and sisters
    are trapped is a hellish cycle of poverty, Lord.
Travelers to third world countries
    witness this pervasive human misery.
We need to use all our energy and resources
    to improve their trying conditions,
    which are so often caused by injustice.
Like me, they deserve to live in dignity,
    with the basic necessities of life.
Help me, Lord, not to look away, not to be blind.
What I do for them, I do for you.
We may always have the poor with us,
    but they need not be destitute.
Good night, Lord.

Holiness

Striving for holiness, Lord,
    is not an option, is it?
Sometimes I'm tempted to wish it were.
Holiness means living in your presence,
    striving for the ideal, reaching for the stars.
It means being single-minded in pleasing you.
If I arrive at the end of life without holiness,
    I will have missed the mark.
I forget, at times, the way I ought to live.
I shrug off the thought, Lord,
    as if holiness were a barrier to a good time.
No one can cast aside your holy will,
    and expect to be pleasing in your sight.
Good night, Lord.

March 9

Refugees

There are millions of people, Lord,
    who have no place to lay their heads,
    because they are refugees.
In Africa, Asia, the Mideast, and Latin America
    entire families and villages are forced
    to flood the roads and take to the seas
    to escape civil (very uncivil) wars,
    famine, earthquakes, and floods.
Grant me a compassionate heart
    and may I not be blind to their suffering.
"I was homeless and you sheltered me"—
    may these words move me to act for them,
    in whom you continue to suffer.
Good night, Lord.

March 10

Good Day

Lord, people often say, "Have a good day!"
They wish me well in my fast-moving world
    where I am submerged in seriousness.
A good day should have some relaxation.
    whether it is a holiday or workday.
Life is not meant to be one giant grindstone.
Do I try to do too much, press too hard, Lord?
Life is what I make it.
Each day may be "good" if I learn to recognize
    your presence in it and find time to relax
    and share a word with you.
As I close my eyes, Lord, I know it has been
    a good day because you have been with me.
Good night, Lord.

Unwinding

This is my favorite time, Lord,
  when the feverish activity is over
  and the pressured moments are past.
There is no need to hurry;
  I am not going anywhere.
Now is the time to unwind,
  to soothe my spirit and imbibe a quiet moment.
The daily frantic pace is dehumanizing,
  like the workers on the stock exchange floor,
  wheeling and dealing in an intense frenzy.
Bless the endlessly busy people, Lord.
May their days be productive
  but may they find peace and contentment.
Good night, Lord.

Humility

Hardly anyone talks about humility any more, Lord.
The saints know there is no other way
  except the way of humility.
The perspective of the proud is off kilter;
  they do not see things accurately,
  least of all, themselves and you, Lord.
Humility is truth, true assessment
  of how things really are, positive or negative.
We kick ourselves at times over blunders,
  knowing they would not have happened
  if we were humble of heart.
Guide my thinking and my judgments, Lord.
Let me be honest with myself and with you.
Good night, Lord.

March 13

Civil Servants

Lord, a cop did me a small courtesy today,
    and as I end this day I am grateful
    for all they do for us every day.
Without them, we would have big problems.
Bless our police officers—men and women:
    detectives, those on the beat, SWAT teams,
    traffic regulators, and chiefs.
We need them to protect us, to control crowds,
    to challenge criminal elements,
    to mediate neighborhood disputes.
Inspire me to appreciate all civil servants,
    and to contribute to harmonious living
    in any way I can—in your name.
Good night, Lord.

March 14

Forgiveness

It takes a special grace to be forgiving, Lord,
    especially when we are really hurt.
No other reaction is acceptable.
We ask so often to be forgiven
    "as we forgive those who trespass against us."
It's a non-negotiable condition.
We are not to seek revenge,
    but even encouraged to pray for those
    who persecute us, to return good for evil.
Peace comes when our bitterness succumbs
    to the sweet concession of forgiveness.
Lord, let me remember this tomorrow:
    It is in pardoning that we are pardoned.
Good night, Lord.

Precious Faith

At the end of the day, Lord,
    as long shadows evaporate in darkness,
    I thank you for all my blessings,
    especially for the religious faith I enjoy.
You are the beginning and the end of my life.
You are my Alpha and the Omega.
How empty my life would be without faith!
How meaningless and insignificant!
Without this faith dimension,
    there is no heaven in sight to guide me,
    no promise of unending joy with you.
You have created me in your image, Lord.
Let me be a person of faith tonight and always.
Good night, Lord.

Media Values

We have become confused about our priorities,
    judging by what we see in the media, Lord.
The good guy in the movie
    is thoroughly depraved—
    dishonest, sleeping around, a user—
    but he's a hero, a role model, and praiseworthy
    because he captures the bad guy.
You and those who speak in your name
    have told us what is of true value,
    what our priorities should be.
Despite life's cloudiness and complications,
    despite the direction the crowd may be marching,
    keep me walking according to your holy will.
Good night, Lord.

March 17

Closer to God

As I settle in for the evening,
  am I closer to you, Lord?
That should be my aim, day after day.
How can I know if I am—
  by my feelings?
That's not a good way, since comforting
  and discomforting feelings are misleading.
Holiness lies in my will, in the awareness
  that I seek you out and try to please you—
  regardless of how I feel about being holy.
It is better, Lord, not to focus on my feelings
  about being close to you,
  but by my determination to embrace your will.
Good night, Lord.

March 18

Truckers

Lots of trucks on the road today, Lord,
  men and women who log mile after mile
  transporting the food and other goods we use.
We can find them troubling when we drive,
  speeding, spraying us on a rainy road.
None of us is independent, though;
  we surely depend on these rigs.
On the open road, inching through city traffic,
  they deliver.
Watch over them, Lord.
May their journeys be safe from accidents and harm.
A good word for our truckers:
  Bless them and their families.
Good night, Lord.

Global Poverty

By comparison, I'm better off, Lord,
　　than the millions of my brothers and sisters
　　in the Third World. In what way?
If First World citizens could travel
　　the Third World, see the daily conditions,
　　no explanation would be necessary.
My brothers and sisters lack the basics:
　　food, clean water, clothing, and shelter.
My lifestyle is several rungs higher.
Lord, what can I do to help them?
Show me how I can help, if not by myself,
　　then in concert with many others
　　to bring about a more just and equitable world.
Good night, Lord.

Daily Dose

We need to eat and drink daily
　　to maintain our strength and life.
We need nourishment for the soul, too.
How fragile our human makeup,
　　that we need a daily dose of contact with you.
Lord, many people schedule quiet moments
　　to read your word in the Bible
　　and to communicate with your Spirit.
Their effort to be in touch is reinforced
　　by prayer and church worship.
Give us this day our daily bread—
　　whatever we need to sustain us in your love
　　and be continually mindful of your presence.
Good night, Lord.

March 21

Illness

When illness strikes, Lord, I turn to you.
A day does not go by
    when I am not reminded of sickness.
Emergency rooms on TV provide high drama.
We drive into town and ambulances race past,
    accelerating toward hospitals.
When I am ill, in pain and distress,
    my thoughts go heavenward.
Doctors are skilled and knowledgeable,
    but they need your blessing, Lord.
Strengthen the patient and medical team
    during illness.
We are all your children.
Good night, Lord.

March 22

Talent

Our creative powers come from you, Lord.
When children display talent, folks ask,
    "Where did he (or she) get it?"
You, Lord, are our heavenly parent, our creator,
 and we get our creativity from you.
We weave words like an exquisite tapestry,
    snatching our breath with our own creativity.
We paint colorful landscapes that invite us
    to enter them for a peaceful stroll.
Sculptures are so lifelike
    we want to reach out and touch them.
These talents enrich our lives, but we
    attribute them to you, to whom be the glory.
Good night, Lord.

Finger Pointing

Hardly a day passes, Lord, when I notice
    something that does not compute.
A serious wrong is taking place
    that may cause harm to others.
Should I look the other way?
Or, should I blow the whistle?
Engineers and contractors know that a structure
    may crumble if they are not on the level.
Does the one who points a finger, Lord,
    promote peace? Well, maybe.
Whistle-blowers often have a hard time.
May I learn to be decisive, to blow the whistle,
    when reason and love demand it.
Good night, Lord.

Selective Thoughts

During waking hours, Lord,
    I think about many things.
My thoughts travel as I travel.
St. Paul has some thoughts about thoughts:
"Your thoughts should be directed
    to all that is true, all that deserves respect,
    all that is honest, pure, admirable,
    decent, virtuous, or worthy of praise."
In short, he tells us, be noble in your thinking.
Let my mind, Lord, move in ideal directions.
May I be as selective in my thoughts
    as I am in choosing books from a library.
Help me to take the high road.
Good night, Lord.

March 25

Students

Lord, bless and help our students.
At this hour, most have closed their books.
Give them patience and perseverance
    as they turn pages and scroll their computers.
But most of all, let them see that their courses
    fit into your master plan,
        that information and knowledge that expressly
        excludes you, Lord, is seriously deficient.
Give them the insight that science
    is simply organized knowledge about your world,
    that the beauty of the arts is a reflection of you.
May their many subjects, from math to cooking,
    lead them to know and love you.
Good night, Lord.

March 26

The Law of Love

Love is more than affection, isn't it, Lord?
It is concretely seeking the good of those
    in our homes, schools, and neighborhoods,
    and around the world.
That's your command, your will, Lord.
You, who love all people unconditionally,
    command us to do likewise.
History shows we aren't doing a good job.
Every century repeats earlier wars, greed,
    bigotry, exploitation, pollution, sexism.
Motivate me, Lord, I pray you,
    to bring about a better tomorrow.
Reverse my selfishness into generous service.
Good night, Lord.

Top of the World

Today began on a high, Lord.
It was one of my "top-of-the-world" days.
Strange about our moods.
We struggle with the elation of the mountains
    and with the gloom of the valleys.
It takes effort to maintain a balanced disposition.
Feeling good is a blessing,
    but when clouds shield the sunshine,
    we need your grace to tough it out.
However I happen to feel tomorrow, Lord,
    keep me in your love.
May I be mindful of your sustaining hand,
    of your divine presence.
Good night, Lord.

Praise and Glory

There is no need, Lord, to try to do
    great things for your benefit.
People may gain worldly acclaim,
    but while everyone is called to serve,
    to contribute to society's progress,
    no one should think that makes you better off.
You, Lord, are the Master of the universe.
You can accomplish what you will.
You do not need any of the things we might do.
How presumptuous to think otherwise.
But wanting to please you, to respect your creation
    renders you praise and glory.
That is enough.
Good night, Lord.

March 29
An Ordered Life

Lord, at the end of this day I think
    about the good intention I had at its start:
    to get my life in order.
Whether it is the garage, the desk, or the closet,
    there is no substitute for good order.
I intend to get the house of our relationship in order,
    yet loose ends remain.
I excuse myself by saying I shouldn't be too tidy;
    that makes people (me) feel uncomfortable.
What I should do is trim the tangents,
    the unneeded details in my relationship with you;
    to whittle down impediments to the union we share.
It means being holy, taking advantage of your grace.
Good night, Lord.

March 30
Sexploitation

It sells, Lord; sex sells.
Has any product been advertised
    not using sex as a lure?
Girlie calendars promote spark plugs.
Your gift of the reproductive process
    is enveloped in the commercial culture.
Too seldom do people object any more.
Once, society had moral restraint, a sense of
    respect, at least an unspoken reverence.
Today we are challenged to follow your call
to be faithful, modest, and chaste.
But for your grace, Lord, we would all wallow
    in the sex culture.
Good night, Lord.

Separated Spouses

Separated people need your blessing, Lord.
Men and women once married
    must be sustained by your strength.
Every day in our fractured society
    we meet friends, relatives, and neighbors
    whose lives have been disrupted.
Wedding marches, once promising melodies,
    have become sour refrains.
Help those whose dreams have been shattered
    to repair the psychological damage,
    and be reunited by your grace.
Watch over them with loving care
    and bless them with renewed confidence.
Good night, Lord.

April 1

Young People

It is good to see young people, Lord.
Youth is not wasted on the young,
  whatever the cynics may say.
They have vitality and curiosity,
  enthusiasm and idealism.
Bless them with inspiring models,
  real-life people who show you love and respect.
May our young men and women, Lord,
  be humble and patient, willing to listen
  to those with more experience and wisdom,
  able to discern what is truly in their best interest.
Our children are your children;
 lead them to their destiny with you.
Good night, Lord.

April 2

Religious Freedom

Religious freedom, Lord—
  I know you wouldn't have it any other way!
Why shouldn't people be free to worship you,
  to engage in a loving relationship with you,
  according to their consciences?
Everyone is free to practice their religion,
  or to practice no religion.
But in the separation of church and state,
  you are excluded from certain areas.
How can we be free when you are banned?
Help us, Lord, to find a way to honor you
  when and where and how we wish
  without offending anyone else.
Good night, Lord.

Perspective

Perspective, Lord!
How do you view the world?
The sun has dipped beyond the rim of Earth,
    but darkness does not dim your vision.
No one grasps the total picture as you do;
    you grasp all creation at a glance.
Blimps take overhead shots of football games,
    science has extended human sight,
    agile computers render virtual reality.
We have come to see things differently now.
We need your grace, Lord, to see the world
    as you see it, through your eyes.
I stand in awe before you, humble.
Good night, Lord.

Security

I am perfectly secure, Lord.
Well, not at every moment.
However, in closing out this day,
    my security is as strong as my trust in you.
My problems have not ceased:
    health, finances, relationships, family.
My life inevitably has crosses to bear.
But you are at my side and hear my prayer.
Nothing, Lord, happens without your will,
    and everything can be transformed
    into your honor and glory.
Security has its foundation in faith and hope.
You are my security, powerful and loving.
Good night, Lord.

April 5
Creation and Science
Science, at times, Lord, may seem
    to be at cross-purposes with my faith.
At the close of this day, I pray
    for all scientists, inventors, and engineers,
    who use your materials for the benefit of all.
They all are engaged with what you provide.
Medicine, physics, chemistry, biology
    all work with your creation,
    new applications of the solids, liquids, and gases
    present from the beginning of time.
I pray that scientific concentration on the created
    will not distract any of us from our Creator,
    in whom there are no contradictions.
Good night, Lord.

April 6
Aging
Lord, everyone is growing older—
    myself included.
It is a process, steady and unstoppable.
As I lie down at the end of the day,
    I thank you for the blessings of my years.
Bless the elderly with graceful aging.
Keep them young at heart,
    full of joy, enthusiasm, and creativity.
There's no substitute for experience, Lord,
    and they have much to offer.
Let them share their wisdom.
For as many years as it pleases you,
    let me serve you with a grateful heart.
Good night, Lord.

My Happiness

Where can I find happiness, Lord?
It has been a good day, maybe a mixed day,
    with highs and lows, good and bad.
Every move I make is in pursuit of happiness.
I seek it in music and song,
    in an ideal spouse.
At times, I charge down wrong paths,
    alluring ways that lead nowhere.
Why? What am I looking for?
Fulfillment, contentment, satisfaction—
    which ultimately must embrace you, Lord,
    the source of all goodness, beauty, and truth.
My soul longs for you.
Good night, Lord.

Insecurity

Some people appear as pillars of strength,
    and I, Lord, am constantly reminded
    of my weakness and insecurity.
At the end of the day I turn to you,
    as a child seeking comfort and approval.
But isn't this good?
Unless I become like a little child,
    I shall not enter your kingdom, Lord.
Confident men and women,
    those "in control"—it is the same for them.
They have to depend on you, without reservation.
If their poise is a facade, it will crumble.
My trust has to be in you. Period.
Good night, Lord.

April 9

Pressure

Pressure, Lord—we've all experienced it.
Some seem to welcome pressure,
    even thrive on it.
Others can't seem to shake it at day's close.
It takes its toll on overly busy people.
Tensions can be unnecessarily homemade.
Deadlines, high expectations, strong demands
    plague us day in and day out.
Computers may facilitate life,
    but they also ensnare and entrap us.
Slow me down, Lord, and teach me to relax.
Make me aware of my limitations
    and teach me the golden norm of moderation.
Good night, Lord.

April 10

Waiting

I did a lot of waiting around today, Lord.
The best planner in the world
    can't avoid unforeseen waiting time.
The car is being repaired.
The doctor has not arrived.
The checkout lines are long.
And traffic is in a gridlock.
"They also serve who only stand and wait."
It's nice to think we accomplish something
    while nursing anxieties and frustrations.
I pray that I may be gracious while waiting.
It can be a special grace to remind me
    of my limitations, and a time to talk to you.
Good night, Lord.

Travel

The travel-tourist industry tantalizes us
　　with attractive pictures of faraway places.
Lord, the lure of the exotic tempts me.
So many places I have not seen:
　　the Statue of Liberty, the Grand Canyon,
　　the White House, and Puget Sound.
I have never been to a horse race, either.
It would be nice, Lord,
　　to see more of your beautiful world.
But if I don't have the time or the money,
　　let me be content with the way things are,
　　or seriously try to plan a trip,
　　or read more about these places.
Good night, Lord.

New Start

A short examination of conscience
　　and a prayer for forgiveness
　　go well with the end of the day, Lord.
I am sorry for my sins and failings.
If I do not acknowledge these,
　　there will be no improvement.
Looking back, seeing my mistakes,
　　I feel like disappearing into oblivion.
Regrettable words, impetuous acts, blind pride—
　　Oh, Lord, how patient you are with me,
　　and how utterly forgiving.
You graciously forgive my contrite soul.
Thanks for the opportunity for a new start.
Good night, Lord.

April 13

My Prayer

The key to communicating with you, Lord,
    is in my heart.
Radio, television, film, fax, press—
    these are unnecessary to speak with you
    as I pray now at day's end.
How good it is to express the peace and joy,
    the anxiety and fear that I feel
    in these quiet moments.
How good to listen to you, Lord.
Grant that I may be open to your voice,
    wherever it may come from,
    the events of the day, the people I meet,
    the papers I read, the movies I see.
Good night, Lord.

April 14

Peace

Let there be peace on earth!
A devout wish, Lord, and a song lyric.
But wishing won't make it so.
Throngs of tourists visit impoverished lands
    and say, "Isn't that too bad,"
    as they travel to luxurious resorts.
If I say "Peace" and smile at a starving person
    without sharing my food, there won't be peace.
Millions go to bed hungry;
    refugees have no shelter.
When will I learn, Lord,
    that if there is to be peace,
    there will first have to be justice?
Good night, Lord.

Discipline

Discipline demands my determination.
I guess I should have tried to put
   a little more into this day, Lord.
I'll get nowhere in my desire to serve you
   unless I make up my mind
   and be willing to pay the price.
Having good intentions is not enough.
"When I have some free time,
   I'll master a foreign language."
Yeah, right.
My motivation has to be high, Lord,
   so that desire becomes deed.
Burn this into my soul.
Good night, Lord.

Love

We thrive on love, Lord.
It really does make the world go round.
We can't survive without it.
How cruel, how useless, how senseless
   to live without the one element
   that makes life what it should be.
We experience love in spouses,
   in nurses tending the sick,
   in public servants uniting society,
   in teachers educating students—
   in endless ways by countless people.
You are the source of our love,
   and infinitely lovable.
Good night, Lord.

Acknowledgment

I passed a trophy shop today, Lord.
"Shall I go in and buy myself one
    to commemorate my accomplishments?"
The thought was good for a laugh.
I would blow my own horn.
Thousands of these awards are bestowed
    to acknowledge what people have done.
Where, Lord, is my trophy for you,
    for you alone do great wonders?
In what way, starting tonight, will I acknowledge
    what you do for me every day?
Whatever is good in this world, in my life,
    I owe to you.
Good night, Lord.

Students

It's ironic, Lord, that once I graduated,
    my appreciation for studies grew.
In school, I thought the studies would never end.
Teachers told us to never stop learning.
Keep my interest high,
    sharpen my curiosity,
    sustain me in my quest to learn.
"Education" means being led somewhere.
Hopefully to you, Lord.
Let history, chemistry, geography, math
    lead to greater comprehension
    of your world, your plan, of you.
Inspire me with the highest ideals.
Good night, Lord.

Boring Teachers

Getting ready for bed, Lord,
I remembered being so bored in school.
Some teachers could make statues yawn.
If there are poor teachers still around,
    I guess I should pray for students.
Give them patience and perseverance, Lord.
May they be mature enough to benefit
    from all teachers, less or more gifted.
Let them see that learning is always possible
    even despite poor teachers.
May their continuing religious studies
    enhance their faith, never be boring,
    and bring them closer to you.
Good night, Lord.

Sacrifice

The sacrifices that people make
    bear witness to their unselfishness, Lord.
As I reflect on those who cross my path each day,
    there is so much to admire:
    parents sacrificing for their families,
    business people putting in 15-hour days,
    people in the military risking their lives.
    missionaries voluntarily living in poverty.
There is no substitute for the spirit of sacrifice.
With it, saints overcome odds
    and sinners reverse their direction.
A silent crucifix preaches eloquently;
    let it teach me to sacrifice.
Good night, Lord.

April 21

Teens

"Why can't they be like we were," Lord,
   "perfect in every way?"
These lyrics about teens are tongue in cheek,
   because we weren't much better,
   and certainly not perfect.
Let me be understanding, Lord,
   to the difficult times they go through.
They need encouragement, not sarcasm.
I pray that these lyrics may temper
   my criticism of maturing teens.
Let me appreciate their qualities,
   their idealism and enthusiasm,
   their generosity and energy.
Good night, Lord.

April 22

New Ideas

New ideas, Lord—let me be slow to ridicule them.
We have seen the incomprehensible,
   the seemingly impossible come true.
Split the atom, make a moon journey,
   send pictures through the air—
   who thought these would be possible?
Let me encourage new ideas, Lord,
   and be open to creative thinking,
   even when it appears dumb at first.
Of course, not every suggestion has merit,
   but treasures are waiting to be discovered.
Let me not disparage a "crazy" idea offhandedly.
Allow me to share in your creativity.
Good night, Lord.

Truth

Uncluttered by preconceptions, Lord,
   children have a fresh, candid,
   unencumbered way of seeing the truth.
Bigotries and prejudices don't clog their minds.
Favor me, I pray, with this childlike attitude,
   to be open and inquisitive and curious.
Bless me with an open mind, to see the truth
   wherever it may be found,
   wherever it may lead.
Truth is liberating;
   it is not to be feared, for it sets me free.
Thanks for the good day
   and for open-minded tomorrows.
Good night, Lord.

Providence

Strange, Lord, how we reflect before retiring;
   we become philosophical or theological.
I don't even know if the stars are out,
   but they are there, thanks to you.
You are aware of them, the sands on the seashore,
   and the hairs on our heads.
You care for the lilies of the field, Lord,
   and the birds of the air.
Help us to look up beyond the galaxies
   and beneath the atoms,
   and know you watch over us.
As the cherished hymn expresses it,
   "How Great Thou Art."
Good night, Lord.

April 25

Interruptions

At times, Lord, life seems to be a giant
    interruption, or inconvenience,
    and there have been more today.
They are inevitable and frustrating.
Friends chat and the phone rings.
Changes in flight times and detours on roads.
The electricity goes off at dinner time.
Neighborhood children play ring-a-lievio
    when we're takng a nap.
All very amusing, were they not irritating.
I need your grace to bear with these,
    live life gracefully,
    and try not to cause these myself.
Good night, Lord.

April 26

Expression

The gift of expression is a blessing, Lord.
I thank you for these articulate people.
They are precise in phrasing, sensitive,
    and imaginative in description.
They know how to come to the point,
    and can do it with forceful emotion.
They are an inspiration to us,
    illustrating beautifully the art of words.
Let them realize the good they can accomplish.
Let the truths they communicate, Lord,
    reflect the nobility of their character.
May they bring glory and honor to you,
    as they bring enjoyment to us.
Good night, Lord.

Liberation

At the end of this day, Lord,
    I count my blessings and thank you.
There are so many less fortunate.
Millions are politically oppressed
    and economically trapped.
Saying that wealth is in the hands of a few
    sounds like the old Communist jargon,
    except that it is true,
    and becoming truer every year.
Let me never become so content, Lord,
    that I turn a blind eye on the hungry,
    the homeless, and the deprived.
Let me not cease to work for their liberation.
Good night, Lord.

Disturbances

Lord, I want to pray for those who disturb me,
    like the time in my travels when a truck
    rumbled by my hotel window at 3 A.M.
How often, Lord, have I been disturbed
    and how often I have disturbed others?
I pray, Lord, for people who have disturbed me,
    not because I like being disturbed,
    but because I want to do what you said.
If I pray only for those who treat me considerately,
    what is that?
For door-slammers and radio blasters,
    for those who cut into lines or tell offensive jokes,
    I pray.
Good night, Lord.

April 29

Unbelievers

Unbelievers, Lord, what makes them tick?
Has no one shared faith with them?
Perhaps people did, but not well
   or gave very bad example,
   or perhaps this is where reason led them.
They might be angry if they knew
   I pray for their conversion.
I'll risk it anyway.
Open their hearts, Lord,
   and let the light of your love shine in.
Let them experience your continuing presence.
Bless atheists and agnostics,
   and strengthen me in my faith.
Good night, Lord.

April 30

Suffering

Why must we suffer, Lord?
It is clear that it is everyone's lot,
   for some more than others.
Is it to bring out the best in us?
To make up for our sins?
Mental anguish, physical pain,
   emotional distress, deprivation—
Some say a compassionate God would not allow this.
Sufferings occur with disorder,
   so their origin is not in you.
Grant this night that I may continue
   to love you and hold on to you
   even through my pain.
Good night, Lord.

Cheerfulness

This morning, Lord, I decided—just like that—
    to be a more cheerful person.
What would make me cheerful?
It's such an effort to sustain cheerfulness
    all my waking hours, non-stop;
    to have a smile for every grouch,
    a chuckle for every complaint,
    a pleasant face for every gloom-sayer.
Those are the external signs, Lord,
    but I have to be content inside.
Let your loving presence be the source
    of my cheerfulness.
I know it will be perfect in the next life.
Good night, Lord.

Golden Rule

I know why there are wars, Lord;
    why there are angry people,
    revengeful persons, vindictive souls!
    why there is so much crime and violence!
People don't treat one another
    the way they want to be treated.
A gross oversimplification, Lord,
    but it's essentially on target.
We have yet to endorse the golden rule
    as the only blueprint for living.
My prayer as I end this day:
    to let this rule guide me in all I do.
Let it be my commitment to love.
Good night, Lord.

May 3

The Giving Lord

How nice to be remembered on our birthdays,
    unwrap presents at Christmas.
Yet, Lord, you say it's better to give than to receive.
I do enjoy giving people gifts,
    but let me not do it to receive praise,
    even your praise, Lord.
Let me do it to express my genuine love,
    because I want to share what I have.
Since goodness tends to spread itself out,
    you created us in your own image
    to give us the best gift you could:
    yourself.
For this I offer you my profound thanks.
Good night, Lord.

May 4

Bereavement

Lord, what does one say to the bereaved
    when they have lost someone to death?
Many are clumsy with words,
    even though the deep sympathy is there.
It helps when relatives and neighbors
    bring food and mind the young children.
"Blessed are they who mourn,
    for they shall be comforted," you told us.
But the loss saddens them and they don't think
    about being comforted later on, Lord.
The hurt is now.
Sustain bereaved families, Lord, and comfort them.
Extend your consoling hand to them.
Good night, Lord.

Blessed Moments

There are blessed moments, Lord,
    when I experience your loving presence.
As I close my eyes for a good night's sleep,
    I think of your reassuring graces.
It is good to savor and cherish them.
Whatever time of year it is, Lord,
    when the icicles hang long
    or when the wildflowers bloom,
    I think, "What a beautiful world."
The earlier stressful anxieties were wastes of time.
I think, instead, of your constant,
    undiminishing love and concern.
Let me never lose sight of your providence.
Good night, Lord.

Need for God

Do I pray best when I'm in trouble, Lord?
Or only when I'm in trouble?
There are anxious moments in any routine day.
Some people, I suspect, pray
    only when they want something from you.
When stomachs are full
    and there are savings in the bank,
    why bother to go to church or pray at all?
By not cultivating a personal relationship
    with you, Lord, I become very shallow.
The truth is—and help me to live by it—
    I have a clear need for you
    in good times and bad.
Good night, Lord.

May 7

Feelings

Sensitivity, feelings, come with creation, Lord,
    and you fashioned us this way for a reason.
Authors, artists, musicians,
    and playwrights thrive on inspiration.
Mothers are on the wavelengths of their children.
Kind souls are motivated by compassion
    for the poor and deprived.
Our feelings need cultivating, discipline,
    channeling, and mastery
    so to direct us in holiness.
By your grace, Lord, may I count my feelings
    as one of your wondrous gifts,
    to enable me to serve you better.
Good night, Lord.

May 8

Close Friend

Praying to you, Lord, is pleasant,
    like chatting with a close friend.
There is no need to shout or repeat,
    because you are right here with me.
Communication is free-flowing and easy.
Even when I struggle to express my feelings,
    you understand.
Our conversation is virtually effortless.
That's the way it is with friends, you and I.
Your holy book warns against thinking
    that prayer will get a hearing
    simply by multiplying words.
How reassuring to know you read my heart!
Good night, Lord.

Success

Lord, it's time to turn in for the day.
Has it been a successful day?
You are the judge.
Some think a day was successful
   if they made a lot of money,
   or if they were seen with important people.
If your will found fulfillment in my efforts,
   I am encouraged, to say the least,
   and would say this day was what it should be.
We tend to judge by externals, Lord;
   you look into the heart.
In the final analysis, my success is measured only
   by how I respond to your grace.
Good night, Lord.

Inspiration

Lord, when "the spirit of God was stirring
   over the waters," when you created the world,
   is this the breath of creativity, inspiration,
   that you share with us?
I wonder about inspiration.
What moves composers to capture
   nature's sounds and the heart's movements?
How do writers come to weave
   colorful words in dazzling phrases?
Is there any true originality but yours, Lord?
Continue to breathe over the waters of our minds.
Let us appreciate the beauty around us,
   your reflected beauty, and be refreshed.
Good night, Lord.

May 11
House of God
"We gather together to sing the Lord's praises."
A hymn recently heard, playing in my mind
 as I retire for the evening.
Houses of God are common in our towns
 where steeples point heavenward
 and bells summon us to worship.
It is your first commandment.
How pleasing, Lord, that we come together,
 brothers and sisters,
  to acknowledge your divinity in public.
Hearts, hands, and voices blend in song and prayer,
 as we affirm that we are one family in faith.
How comforting it is to pray to you together.
Good night, Lord.

May 12
Priorities
I need your help, Lord, as I try
 to bluster through life at a hurried pace.
We Americans want it done yesterday.
There are many opportunities to distinguish
 the more important from the less important.
The demands of bureaucracies and legalities,
 the ordinary complications of daily living,
 all require the soothing balm of patience.
Jamming the day and crowding the hours
 does not always spell progress.
With all these challenges, I need your grace
 to be balanced about my priorities.
Let me see these demands through your eyes.
Good night, Lord.

The Poor

My conscience bothers me at times, Lord.
I guess you know that.
It flares up when the poor come into sight,
    especially when television and magazines
    carry images of the struggle for existence.
Men, women, and children by the millions
    live in squalor, jammed into barrios.
As sophisticated as some countries have become,
    it does not appear that there is a resolve
    to help our brothers and sisters.
Am I part of the problem, Lord, because I am
    not sufficiently engaged in its solution?
Love conquers all.
Good night, Lord.

Children

Good parents set a positive example, Lord.
Every day, we see caring mothers and fathers.
You are as concerned as they are, even more.
You send angel guardians to guide their steps.
Lord, you love their innocence and purity.
"Woe to those who lead little ones astray,"
    you told us.
Conscientious parents are a light to the young.
But it's impossible to shield their eyes and ears
    from all temptation.
Bless all children with parents who communicate
    that your holy will sets the standard.
Bless parents with children who will respect them.
Good night, Lord.

May 15

Convictions

"Don't even think of parking here"—
   that's what the sign said.
The message was unmistakable: no indecision!
Isn't that the way it ought to be, Lord,
   when it comes to personal convictions?
Physical strength and vigor are important,
   but inside strength is indispensable.
Trial, hardship, challenge must not deter me.
If I set my sights set on lofty goals,
   I can live by my convictions,
   which means living by your holy will.
My spirit is willing,
   but you are my inside strength.
Good night, Lord.

May 16

Praying for Others

People ask for prayers, Lord.
How often men and women have asked
   that I speak to you on their behalf!
At times their requests are fervent, even desperate.
They want many voices storming heaven.
I, too, have asked others to pray for me,
   begged for their intercession.
There are problems: people, money, health—
   the usual difficulties in life, Lord.
We help one another, sharing the burden,
   carrying the heavy load of life.
There is comfort in mutual support.
Hear our prayers, I pray you.
Good night, Lord.

God's Presence

Paul provides a powerful one-liner, Lord:
    "If God is for us, who can be against us?"
It's good to reflect on this
    when things become challenging.
With you on our side, Lord,
    failure is not possible
Insurance companies can't offer greater assurance.
It's repeated over and over in the Bible.
Calamities may be great, obstacles formidable,
    but nothing overcomes the power of your love.
I do not walk alone, Lord—
    now that's a comforting line.
Your people enjoy your divine providence.
Good night, Lord.

Wisdom

Bless me with wisdom, Lord.
In reviewing the day, I realize
    that not all my decisions were wise.
Solomon, favored with the ability to discern,
    was famous for his wisdom.
Would that everyone could share in his blessing!
Wisdom teaches perspective, how to see events
    unfolding according to your plan.
Wisdom teaches good human relations,
    how to cultivate respect,
    understanding, and tolerance.
You, Lord, are the source of wisdom.
May we be wise according to your thought.
Good night, Lord.

May 19

Articulation

"Have something to say, and say it."
Articulation is not always that easy, Lord.
At times there's a chasm between our thoughts
    and how we express ourselves.
Children lack the vocabulary to explain.
Wives struggle to broach
    sensitive subjects with husbands.
Writers and diplomats search for phrases
    and preachers are misunderstood.
And misunderstandings lead to conflict.
Help me to communicate
    with the people in my life.
It is a good thing that you can read my mind.
Good night, Lord.

May 20

Economy

The economy, Lord, is a high concern,
    perhaps the dominating subject.
We talk about debt, real estate, and interest rates.
In supermarkets and malls we watch prices go up,
    as the real value of paychecks goes down.
Some fathers work two jobs, and mothers, too.
This quest for funds becomes overwhelming.
    affecting our relationships.
It can be quite consuming to the human spirit,
    a threat to our peace of mind.
We remind ourselves that the lilies of the field
    and the birds of the air are in your hands.
You are our God, not money.
Good night, Lord.

Search for Meaning

Every day I see people in the search for meaning.
Lord, what is the significance of life?
Movies, novels, and television generally
    fail to provide much insight.
Men and women butterfly from job to job,
    from relationship to relationship,
    even from marriage to marriage.
How many career changes can we have?
Happy are those, Lord, who've learned that our
    hearts will rest when they have rested in you,
    that you created us to love and serve you.
You are not only the promise of paradise,
    but are the very reason for my existence.
Good night, Lord.

Respect

At times I'm really tempted, Lord,
    to lash out at those who irritate me.
As I close my eyes for the day,
    I realize that you love troublemakers.
Whether I like it or not, I have to treat
    hostile or annoying people with respect.
Those who bug me or even injure me
    do not gain merit for what they did.
Still, Lord, you love them in spite of all.
You see in them, as you do in me,
    the potential for conversion.
The worst can bring out the best in us.
Can I do better than follow your lead?
Good night, Lord.

May 23

Humility

A humble disposition wins friends, Lord.
No one loves an arrogant person.
Examining my conscience before retiring
   makes me realize I can hide nothing from you.
It's your paradox, Lord, to put down the mighty
   and to exalt the lowly.
Humility is truth, and, with your grace,
   I can accept a realistic picture of myself.
This is not a false pride, denying my talents,
   minimizing them unrealistically.
It is a disposition to see myself as you do.
I can shoot for the moon and, if I arrive,
   attribute all to you.
Good night, Lord.

May 24

Kidding

An awful lot of kidding goes on, Lord,
   some good-natured; some mean-spirited.
It's hard to avoid all offense;
   I mean, some people are very sensitive.
Would-be comedians want to say something funny.
Accent, girth, large noses, bald heads, social status—
   these are the targets.
Are they attempting to build themselves up
   by putting others down? What price a laugh?
Help me to be good-natured and gracious
   in the face of needling and humorous jibes.
Help me also, to be mindful of others' feelings
   when I am tempted to kid them.
Good night, Lord.

Good Cheer Messengers

Bless messengers of good cheer, Lord,
    these smiling, good-natured people
    who put a positive spin on life.
With challenges on all fronts,
    we can use all the good news we can get.
The media often focuses on the bizarre
    and the negative, Lord,
    disasters, accidents, wars, crimes.
These facts of life have a cumulative effect,
    like a gathering storm blocking the sunshine.
We have a wonderful country, one to be proud of.
We believe in you, Lord;
    help us to believe in ourselves.
Good night, Lord.

Reconciliation

Help me, Lord, to be reconciled
    with all the people in my life.
Tonight, it strikes me that we are contentious.
We must make a continual effort
    to maintain our relationships.
Who has not been crossed or provoked?
Reconciliation has to do with you, Lord,
    since your forgiveness is conditioned
    on our forgiveness of others.
If I want to be free interiorly,
    I must seek it by forgiving others
    and seeking it for myself.
Give me the good grace to heal broken relationships.
Good night, Lord.

Inside Line

Some think priests, nuns, deacons
    have an inside line, Lord;
    a hotline to heaven, so to speak.
I certainly hope the channels are used a lot.
But you are receptive to everyone.
There are no office hours; the door always open.
Who else but you, Lord, is so available,
    so receptive and responsive?
Your interest is in each person individually,
    and your love is limitless;
You are only a prayer away.
It's always nice talking with you;
    we'll do it again soon.
Good night, Lord.

Blundering Through

Lord, you've heard of Fort Blunder,
    on Lake Champlain, a fort renamed
    because it was the site of a big mistake?
We all make errors, but none so monumental.
Despite our limitations and occasional stupidity,
    the world does not come crumbling down.
No one is perfect but you, Lord.
Somehow, in your providence,
    you even bring benefit from our mistakes.
Give us the grace to go forward with courage,
    knowing that mistakes will be made.
Let us be sincere, invoke the Holy Spirit,
    and shoot the works.
Good night, Lord.

Why

The knowledge we acquire, Lord,
    filters through the learning process,
    much like a soft rain sinks into a thirsty earth.
And still, mysteries remain and we ask why:
    accidents, calamities, devastating events.
We ask how they fit in with your loving plan.
We search long for reasons in the labyrinth
    of life's experiences,
    as children beleaguer parents for answers.
I must trust in you, Lord,
    even when, or because, I don't understand.
I never question your love, though.
May your glory be enhanced by my endurance.
Good night, Lord.

Guiding Light

The psalmist says, "The Lord's precepts are right,
    rejoicing the heart!"
Many times, though, people think your commandments
    are restrictive, cramping their style.
They give us reason to rejoice, Lord,
    because they guide us along the way
    and lead us to you.
They are a great blessing, a guiding light.
Lord, they are a far-reaching lighthouse beam
    stretched across troubled waters.
I must chase ill-founded resentment
    from my heart and embrace your will
    as I find it in commandments—ten and more.
Good night, Lord.

May 31

God's Revelation

Variety is the spice of life, Lord,
    and our wondrous world brims with flavor.
As I close this day, I am enriched by your world.
Like the poet,
    "O world, I cannot hold thee close enough."
The grace of gulls gliding over silvery waters,
    the charm of wildflowers coloring a hillside,
    the rugged beauty of seaside cliffs,
    a spider weaving a web.
They are a revelation of you, Lord, the Divine Artist.
So are the poets, songwriters, and other artists
    who unravel the beauty of human nature.
May this world and I
    praise and glorify you forever.
Good night, Lord.

Flowers

Gardeners and florists color our lives, Lord,
with flowers that make the land sing.
They produce riots of reds and yellows
and lavenders and pinks.
They arrange sprays and bouquets to gladden
the hearts of those entering wedlock.
They bring comfort and solace to those
saddened by death and separation.
There are buds and blossoms
for the sick and confined.
Gardenias and gladiolas, roses and chrysanthemums
decorate your altars as signs of love and respect.
Bless those who communicate such joy in our lives.
Good night, Lord.

Freedom

There is much talk about freedom, Lord,
but not everyone means the same thing.
I appreciate my freedom,
despite the widespread confusion.
St. Peter advised us to live free,
but not to misuse our freedom
as a passport for permissiveness.
Let me use my freedom well, Lord,
to be free to do as I ought.
Let me be free to obey your holy will,
to cherish the guidelines of your precepts.
You determine the standards;
not to follow them is my undoing.
Good night, Lord.

June 3
Hospital Patients
Bless the patients in hospitals, Lord;
    they need to know that you love them.
Some get around to serious thoughts about you.
They may have neglected you, ignored you,
    pretended you do not exist.
Now, perhaps a little apprehensive,
    they turn to you, Lord,
    and begin to pray again.
Physical illness can be an occasion
    for nourishing their spiritual health.
Grant courage to all those confined
    and let them grow closer to you.
Strengthen all of us in our challenges.
Good night, Lord.

June 4
Immigrants
Suppose I was an immigrant, Lord;
    how fearful to arrive in a new land.
Customs, language, and laws would be strange.
So many newcomers arrive from Asia, Africa, Europe,
    and Latin America.
Refugees by the millions dream of migrating
    to this country of promise.
Help us, Lord, to cultivate a receptive atmosphere.
Our ancestors spoke Chinese, Italian, and Greek.
We are enriched by the diversity and the vitality
    of new friends and neighbors.
"I was a stranger and you welcomed me."
Let me welcome these strangers, in your name.
Good night, Lord.

Parents of Teenagers

Bless the parents of teenagers, Lord.
Tonight, these parents have formidable challenges.
Their lovely children grow into adolescence and,
     at times, a period of bewilderment and confusion.
They acquire new friends
     and a variety of powerful influences.
There are parties and proms, rallies and outings.
Parents teach them how to fly,
     like birds from the nest,
     but they aren't always certain of the direction.
Guide these parents, Lord, and show them your love.
Let them see they were once their children's age.
Give them patience, peace, and understanding.
Good night, Lord.

Chronic Complainers

I pray for those who wear me down: complainers.
They appear to be stuck in low gear,
     grinding out silly gripes profusely.
They seem to be content
     in their characteristic discontentment.
They've developed a habit of seeing the downside
     and the dark side of everything.
Inspire them to see the sunny side of situations.
No one should be so consistently displeased.
Finding faults becomes ingrained.
May they search for rainbows on rainy days.
And help me, Lord, to count my blessings
     and rejoice in my good fortune.
Good night, Lord.

June 7
A Good World
There is much good in the world
   and you are aware of it, Lord, I know.
Thinking back on the day, I see smiling faces,
   courteous people, and kind neighbors.
The bad guys get all the attention,
   the lead stories in the media.
A small percentage of the socially offensive
   make misery in proportion far beyond their numbers.
It is encouraging to note dedicated doctors
   and bus drivers, architects, and mechanics.
A great many people are cheerful, self-sacrificing,
   respectful, and conscientious.
We are all blessed by the goodness of many hearts.
Good night, Lord.

June 8
Executives
I am moved to pray for corporate executives, Lord.
Some people ask why because they are
   so amply paid and enjoy special benefits.
They operate in luxurious offices
   and ride to work in limousines.
Their jobs may look easy, as you know,
   but they bear awesome responsibilities.
Give them wisdom and interior peace, Lord.
Their decisions affect the lives of many.
Let them be humble, which is precious in your sight.
May their success be based on the lasting good
   they accomplish for their employees,
   not only on the bottom line.
Good night, Lord.

Overweight

No one knows the burden of overweight people
    like those who have experienced it, Lord.
Many of us have gone through the ordeal,
    or are still engaged in the battle.
Chubby children find themselves full-bodied
    through no fault of their own.
There is a feverish craze today, Lord,
    to acquire a perfect body, like the model's,
    but happiness is not a slim torso.
Let us hold to a healthy diet and exercise
    and realize that no one has gained heaven
    simply because they were pencil thin!
Grant us clear-headed priorities.
Good night, Lord.

Captives

Captive people are pretty much out of sight, Lord,
    but not out of mind, at least not yours.
Many are behind bars because they are dangerous,
    but there are thousands more held unjustly
    and deprived of their human rights
    because of their political views.
Lord, give them strength and courage
    and enhance their hope for release.
Look with favor on internees in degrading prisons,
    detained because of their religion.
Embrace those undergoing torture.
As you caused Peter's chains to fall from his limbs,
    so set all these captives free.
Good night, Lord.

June 11

New Thoughts

Refresh my mind with new thoughts, Lord.
Weary as I am after this long day,
    inspire my mind with creative ideas.
Help me to rethink ordinary things,
    to see them in a different light,
        observe them from a different perspective.
Lord, may I never fail to appreciate
    the potential at my finger tips.
Let me reassess my own little corner of the world.
Focus my inner vision to discover hidden beauty,
    to appreciate family and friends,
        to comprehend your limitless love.
Quicken my being with your life.
Good night, Lord.

June 12

Happy Birthday

Lord, people the world over sing "Happy Birthday."
They commemorate the great event
    of emerging from their mother's womb.
It is an important anniversary for the young
    and old who celebrate their birth.
Grant them health, happiness, and renewed joy.
May each birthday bring us closer to one another,
    and especially to you, Lord, the giver of life.
Birth is a blessing for mothers who welcomed
    and then nurtured the new life.
It is a blessing for fathers.
It is a blessing for each of us as individuals,
    as unique, distinct persons loved by you.
Good night, Lord.

Special Teachers

I pray for a blessing on parents and teachers
    of the developmentally disabled, Lord!
What a career and vocation they have!
Caring for physically handicapped persons
    and for retarded people is a unique calling.
These are your children in a special way.
They have an unusual gift to give us,
    often without any pretense or guile.
These special people sometimes put us to shame
    with their simplicity and friendliness,
        their patience and courage.
Bless those who care for them and teach them.
Your grace is sufficient for them.
Good night, Lord.

Politicians

Politicians, Lord, do they need a helping hand?
They are full of platitudes before election.
Bless them, for they need wisdom and moral strength,
    and an attitude of servanthood.
These are the men and women who feel
    they have ideas and leadership qualities.
Lord, assist them in being unselfish in the noble pursuit
    of making this a better world.
Make them strong under the pressure of interest groups
    working against the common good.
I pray that they may always be sensitive
    to the needs of the poor and the neglected.
Aid them in defining correct public policy.
Good night, Lord.

June 15

Music Students

Tonight, Lord, my mind is on those who brighten
    our lives, especially musicians.
Music contributes so much to our happiness,
Bless budding musicians, Lord, who some day
    may play or compose beautiful music for us.
Sustain the efforts of those struggling with the trumpet,
    the piano, and the harp.
Perseverance may be painful for the cellist, the flutist,
    and the sax player.
There may be some agony involved for the instructors
    and uninvolved listeners, too.
May they praise you in churches and concert halls,
    in parades, night clubs, and dance halls.
Good night, Lord.

June 16

Challenge of Loving

Is there really any other challenge in life, Lord,
    except to be loving?
Are not all our relationships reduced to,
    based on, doing good?
The day is spent, Lord, but I feel I should
    have done more today,
    that I missed opportunities to show love.
The world is filled with rejection and violence,
    with unkind words and injustice.
Millions of our brothers and sisters are trapped
    in the cycle of grinding poverty.
There is no solution except to love unreservedly—
    as you do.
Good night, Lord.

Lived Convictions

Lip service won't win an eternal crown,
    will it, Lord?
We have fast talkers in our world,
    but they can't con you.
Not all who call out "Lord, Lord"
    will enter the kingdom
    but only those who do the will of the Father.
Words winged to heaven without substance
    and sincerity are empty.
Give us the courage of our convictions, Lord,
    to put our actions where our mouths are
    that we may live what we profess.
May your will be done with daily deeds.
Good night, Lord.

Laughter

What would a home be, Lord,
    without the sound of laughter?
How about church, at worship? There, too?
Preachers who are lighthearted on occasion
    create a more receptive mood.
People with a sense of humor are more balanced;
    their seriousness is tempered.
Children are usually filled with laughter,
    and are we not all your children?
Is it not true that unless we become like little children,
    we shall not enter the kingdom?
Help us to lighten the load of the heavily burdened,
    and this has to include ourselves.
Good night, Lord.

June 19

Will Power

Will power, Lord, takes us out of neutral
    and gets us into gear.
Those blessed with lesser talents compensate
    with the force of their wills, their motives.
The handicapped—blind, deaf, immobile, retarded—
    they show us the way.
They make significant contributions
    in science, literature, and human relations.
They are "can do" people
    who show us that "it can be done."
Help us sinners to see that it is possible
    to climb out of the pits and to repent.
Together with your grace, will power succeeds.
Good night, Lord.

June 20

Time

The clock has ticked away
    since I rose this morning, Lord.
How time races past us or drags by painfully.
Understanding time gives us a handle on life.
And appreciating it may enable us to serve you better.
The human heart beats millions of times
    from the womb through the declining years.
We are on a spin, travelers through time—
    long or short.
Help me, Lord, to live up to my potential
    and use well the time you will allot me.
May I praise you while there is time
    and realize that my time is your time.
Good night, Lord.

Ostrichlike

Lord, at times I fail to recognize reality around me.
I bury my head in the sand, like an ostrich.
I say, "I didn't know that,"
    and people retort, "You should have known."
If my vision is limited through my own fault,
    I am accountable.
Closing my eyes to glaring injustice,
    hardly noticing starving millions,
    that's putting my head in the sand.
Open my eyes, Lord, so I may see the reality around me,
    not just in far-off places.
Open my heart so I may respond lovingly.
And may I never fail to acknowledge you.
Good night, Lord.

Innocence

There is nothing so charming, Lord,
    as a child's face.
Lord, isn't that their innocence shining through?
Innocence means we live in your love.
We have not broken our friendship by sinning.
Sin isn't discussed much these days;
    there appears to be a huge cover-up,
    an attempt to justify immorality.
None of us can become children again, Lord,
    but by your grace we can remain childlike.
Children have no guile, seem incapable of deception;
    their innocence mirrors spiritual beauty.
Inspire us to strive for such innocence.
Good night, Lord.

June 23
Forgetting About Self
When I am sad and weary, Lord,
   it's time to make someone else happy.
It's an age-old lesson to change thought direction.
The focus, then, is not on me and my depression,
   but on the elderly, handicapped, home-bound.
It is in giving that we receive, as Francis said.
It's one of those paradoxes, Lord.
If I am lonely and cannot sleep,
   it's time to plan on visiting a hospital.
Maybe go to a nursing home, or to a group home
   for the retarded or paraplegics.
Their smiles and cordiality will tell me
   to think of others more than I do.
Good night, Lord.

June 24
Overly Sensitive
If I have offended anyone today, Lord,
   I am very sorry,
   especially for overly sensitive people.
All of us are sensitive, but some more so
   and they are hurt more easily.
Who welcomes tactless remarks about being too heavy,
   or about having bad teeth or bald heads?
We might provoke someone when we kid them
   about their accents or their clothes.
Help those who overreact to a well-meant jibe.
Bless us all, Lord, with the grace to grin and bear
   comments not entirely welcomed.
Let me bear them gracefully.
Good night, Lord.

Law

Lord, honesty is still the best policy, isn't it,
    benefitting us all?
I'm relaxing at the end of the day,
    trying to make sense of life's details.
All your commandments are eminently practical.
They make for good order.
People who resent your laws, Lord,
    don't see how much they profit from them.
Lawbreakers cause our insurance rates to rise.
Taxpayers demand greater protection,
    and who pays for the service?
You love us, Lord, and so you give us direction.
Wouldn't obedience cost less and provide more?
Good night, Lord.

Optimism

Optimism depends on how big a God we believe in.
Lord, those who truly know you are blessed
    with a confidence money can't buy.
Let me be convinced of your personal interest,
    your all-embracing love.
A deep faith sustains me through life's negatives,
    the storms of discouragement and heartache.
A strong belief, an indestructible trust in you, Lord,
    secures my unflappable relationship with you.
A true believer is a positive person.
There's no cross that will overcome me
    if I am grounded in your grace.
Let my faith and optimism continue to grow.
Good night, Lord.

June 27

Keeping Score

Some folks, Lord, don't expect you to keep score,
    but they do speak about some book
    where deeds are recorded, good and bad.
We are so into record-keeping, being exact.
Spectators are outraged if the home team
    is deprived of seconds on the game clock.
Computers at checkouts have to be accurate,
    tax payments exact, interest rates precise.
Why are we so demanding of ourselves in this way,
    but uncaring about the one score that matters?
It's good for me to know the score,
    that I must love you and others,
    but let you do the scorekeeping.
Good night, Lord.

June 28

Waste

Haste makes waste; waste makes want;
    and want makes woe.
Strange, Lord, how slogans fly into our heads,
    especially when going to sleep.
We waste while others want—tons of food in restaurants
    and in home kitchens while millions starve.
Some overstock their wardrobes,
    while the poor are cold and wear rags.
We speed and consume fuel as if it were water,
    while others have to walk even to fetch water.
Conservation is a positive word;
    practicing it can lead to sharing the goods we have.
We may be getting the hang of it, with our recycling.
Good night, Lord.

Science Fiction

Science fiction really fascinates us, Lord;
    we love aliens and life on other planets.
Imagination and high tech develop special effects:
    robots, ET creatures, and space stations.
Some day we may find that science fiction
    is not just wild imaginings, after all.
In any event, Lord, it is important to acknowledge
    you as Creator and Master of the Universe.
Anything less belies the truth
    and denies you the glory you deserve.
For now, I must keep my feet on the ground
    and honor you as I know how.
My mind may be in space, but I live on earth.
Good night, Lord.

Renewal

Renew my spirit, Lord.
You invited me to come to you, to pray,
    when my life becomes burdensome.
Sleep recharges my batteries,
    and I look forward to restful hours.
As upbeat as I try to be, my spirit is willing,
    but my flesh is sometimes weak, Lord.
Soul and body are a single unit
    and one influences the other.
Fire my imagination, activate my potential,
    so that ordinary tasks do not wear me out.
For those who love you,
    everything works together for a greater good.
Good night, Lord.

July 1
Family Harmony
How sweet it is, Lord, when people live in harmony.
Bless family members so that they may make
    beautiful music together at home.
Let their communication be open, loving.
Strengthen the marriage bond.
Help the children to honor their parents, Lord,
    and confide in them.
May discord and strife never overcome them.
Let their conversations be occasions of joy.
May kind words refresh their minds and hearts.
Let each person make a positive contribution
    by generosity and unselfishness.
You are the unseen member of all families.
Good night, Lord.

July 2
Widowed and Divorced
Lord, look with favor on the widowed and divorced.
They suffer the trauma and tragedy of lost love,
    a bewildering turn in life.
As life's journey becomes confusing,
    they search for meaning.
May they find peace in prayer, Lord,
    and comfort in their relationship with you.
Banish all bitterness from their hearts.
May their minds and hearts turn to you
    in the crucible of fate that they endure.
Nothing is permitted in your providence
    that cannot be transformed into good.
You are not far from us; your grace is sufficient.
Good night, Lord.

Expectant Parents

Families are close to your heart, Lord.
Fathers and mothers look forward
    to the birth of their children.
The expectation of a new child brings joy.
There are baby clothes to purchase, child care
    books to read, birthing classes to attend.
And there is prayer, entreating you, Lord,
    for wisdom and guidance to be good parents.
New arrivals bring challenge,
    and a new dimension to the family.
Inspire them to realize that their mission
    is to lead their offspring to you.
Enhance their happiness in their sharing of life.
Good night, Lord.

Marriage

Lord, you call married couples to bear witness
    to their love for each other and for you.
They declare this publicly at your altar.
Romantic songs suggest that it is possible
    to see love in their eyes,
    to hear love in their sighs.
But, united by you, Lord, they are to be signs
    of self-giving and fidelity.
Theirs is a daily opportunity to grow in grace,
    to mature as persons.
Bless them as they meet the challenges
    in their lifelong relationship.
Grant them the grace to fulfill their calling.
Good night, Lord.

July 5

Family

Lord, love is not merely many-splendored,
    but also a permanent arrangement.
We are not supposed to fall out of love.
Like you, Lord, who are so magnanimous,
    we are not to reject each other.
Bless family relationships, Lord, with your grace.
Bless brothers and sisters, relatives and cousins,
    husbands and wives whose union
    comes under so much stress.
If one offends, let the other offer pardon.
Teach them the true meaning of love,
    which is kind, patient, and long-suffering.
It makes things right and heals the heart's wounds.
Good night, Lord.

July 6

Grace

Lord, how many people this evening are
    on the verge of doing the wrong thing?
I know well each day has its temptations.
Some people this moment may be leaning
    toward doing what is immoral
    or toward not doing what is moral.
Nudged by the bad example of others,
    they are about to decide, Lord,
    declaring their defiance of your holy will.
Flood their souls with your grace so that they
    may change their minds, alter their attitudes.
I pray that they—and I—may always
    be mindful of your presence.
Good night, Lord.

Interfaith Marriage

In this religiously divided world, Lord,
  it is common that men and women of
  different religions will fall in love.
Not everyone prays with the same convictions.
Bless all couples of mixed faith, Lord,
  who are united in loving commitment.
Help them to anticipate the serious challenges
  of compatibility.
May the devotion each has to you prosper
  through their good example.
And may their children not be reared
  in an atmosphere of indifference.
May each find you along the paths you show them.
Good night, Lord.

Hearty Laughter

Lord, bless those with hearty laughs
  and a sense of humor.
In the release of cheerful expression,
  they charge the atmosphere
  with much needed relaxation.
Weighted with worry, they cast their burden aside
 with hearty laughter
  and lift the spirits of others.
It is therapy for a charged-up environment.
Lord, strengthen those who know how to laugh
  and temper a grim atmosphere.
Give them an even greater trust in you,
  a deeper confidence in your watchful care.
Good night, Lord.

July 9

The Right Thing

Bless us, Lord, as we ride the seesaw of life.
We often totter on the brink of decision,
   wavering, hesitating, and straddling
   the fence of moral decision.
Shall we, or not?
"Well, it's my life and I'll live it the way I want,"
   we tell ourselves.
We are tempted to seize the moment
   and disregard the consequences.
Strengthen our will power, Lord.
We praise and honor you
   when we deny ourselves for a greater good.
Let all our decisions be good ones—in your name.
Good night, Lord.

July 10

Forgiveness

Lord, as I pray to you this evening,
 I feel so low I hesitate to look up—
   and see you, my loving God.
I have been wicked, selfish in many ways.
Help me not to forget how much
   you love me, even when I sin.
You do not turn your back on me, Lord,
   but look for the return of your prodigal child.
Grant me a true change of heart, repentance.
You have prepared a feast for the day
   I beg your pardon.
Forgiveness is a sweet word,
   spoken by a merciful God.
Good night, Lord.

Cheerful Giver

Lord, you love a cheerful giver.
How pleasant to serve you with a smile,
   to give and not to count the cost.
Love is the will to do good, a powerful motivation.
There is happiness in doing kind deeds,
   joy in generosity.
To serve you reluctantly, begrudgingly,
   grinds all enthusiasm to a halt.
Let me not keep score in serving you, Lord,
   as a calculating minimalist,
   but travel the extra mile willingly,
   no matter the effort required.
Help me to think positively, to respond graciously.
Good night, Lord.

Dependence

Lord, fashion my inmost being.
I need your grace.
As I close out my day with prayer, I realize
   that even my thoughts depend on you.
What can I do without you?
It is mysterious how free I am,
   yet so dependent on you.
Grant me an open disposition of mind and heart,
   eager and receptive to your gifts.
You have blessed me with the gift of life.
You are the source of my existence—
   the way, the truth, and life itself.
Thank you for all you are and all you give.
Good night, Lord.

July 13

Always Thankful

Lord, I pray tonight that I may live my days
    in a constant state of gratitude.
Thanks for all the blessings of this day.
May I never grow weary of thanking you
    and praising you for your gifts.
What do I have that I have not received?
You are the giver of all gifts, even those bestowed
    by freely giving persons.
I confess I was not always so enlightened
    to recognize your sustaining hand.
You watch over us with tender, giving care.
You make me feel like a V.I.P.,
    enjoying favored status.
Good night, Lord.

July 14

Awesome People

Lord, I am in awe of certain people.
They do what would be impossible for me:
    scholars, athletes, explorers, politicians.
They are specialists who have honed
    their skills to perfection.
Some assemble highly technical machines;
    others do research in medicine and science;
    they author books—all making wonderful
    and lasting contributions to society.
How good it is to have such qualified,
    dedicated men and women
    whose work exacts long hours and diligent study.
May their motives be for the good of humankind.
Good night, Lord.

Real and Imaginary

Lord, help us to distinguish reality and sham,
    the real world from make-believe,
    the essence of a thing from its glossy cover,
    truth from its many disguises.
From our most tender years, we are exposed
    to myths, fairy tales, and fantasies.
We are reared in an environment heavily laden
    with the imagined and what is not actual.
Grant us the gift of discernment so that
    we may filter all we come in contact with
    and recognize which is which.
May the judgments we make lead us
    to the one, the good, the beautiful—you!
Good night, Lord.

Divine Patience

I have to tell you, Lord, that some people
    try my patience no end.
They nearly drive me up a wall.
Why can't they get orders straight?
Assignments are bungled; ordinary tasks muffed;
    instructions are disregarded, lateness abounds.
They have other ideas about how to do jobs.
Then, Lord, at times like this . . .
    I think of my own mistakes and failings
    and I think of your patience with me,
Remembering my own mistakes settles me down.
How trying it must be for you
    to witness my pride and foolishness.
Good night, Lord.

July 17

Overextended

Some people go crazy with credit cards, Lord.
They forget that plastic means money.
They'd be more restrained if they had
    to plunk down twenties instead.
With all the calculators and computers around,
    you'd think no one would be overextended.
Yet families are deep in debt and want to borrow more.
I'm sure other factors enter in, Lord,
    such as wagering and imprudent squandering.
Help us to be good stewards of what we have,
    spending wisely and investing responsibly,
    and not to spend what we don't have.
It's a way to honor and praise you.
Good night, Lord.

July 18

Creativity

Lord, patterned after your image and likeness,
    we share your creativity.
The chef declares a new dish is coming to mind.
A song writer hears a melody in her head.
A writer longs to see scrolling pages
    of adventure, romance, and intrigue.
A florist envisions a colorful, new arrangement.
An architect is inspired with a new design.
Activate all our potential, Lord, that we may
    create an even more attractive world.
You have entrusted us with Planet Earth.
Grant that we may refine its resources
    for your eternal praise and glory.
Good night, Lord.

Moderation

Let us recognize our limitations, Lord,
    and make moderation the rule of thumb.
Some folks edge themselves beyond self-control
    and call for "one for the road."
Macho and bravado, today's rallying calls,
    are not so desirable as a humble spirit
    that knows when to say "enough."
More is less, every time.
We must not fear to be honest with ourselves.
Giving a maximum effort for a good cause
    is not the same as imprudent excess.
It's just common sense to pace ourselves
    and recognize that virtue lies in the middle.
Good night, Lord.

Early Birds

Now that the sun has set, Lord,
    and night is gaining on us,
    I think of early morning anchors.
Besides keeping us up on the news and weather,
    they flavor our day.
Bless those, Lord, who choose music and song
    that make us glad we are awake, alive.
They enrich our lives with lively imagination
    and facile tongue.
They package chatter and good cheer
    and launch us on our way to work.
Making life pleasant for others is a noble pursuit.
What can I do each day to take up this challenge?
Good night, Lord.

July 21

Upbeat

The psalmist speaks about praising you, Lord,
   with the lute, lyre, and harp.
 I'll bet you like music with a little pep to it.
Church music is beautiful and reverent;
   sometimes it slips into the solemn and sober.
Traditional churchgoers seem to insist that
   a hushed atmosphere is more conducive
   to communicating with you, Lord.
Carefree children, though, skip through their days
   accompanied by light and lively music.
Let us be open to different kinds of music;
   each has its place if it lifts the heart
   in song and praise to you.
Good night, Lord.

July 22

Music

Music primes the pump, Lord.
When our feet stomp to the beat,
   our whole being comes alive.
We'll have to go a long way
   to improve on this therapy.
It's a joy to start the day with a happy note,
   and, later, when we have unwound,
   to let music soothe our weariness.
Stimulating melodies and rhythmic measures
   rank high in lifting our spirit.
This, Lord, is one of your great blessings.
Thanks for all your gifts, especially music,
   which tells us something about you.
Good night, Lord.

Cemeteries

Cemeteries are everywhere, Lord.
It's good to live near one or to visit one;
    they make us think and feel.
Tombstones mark the resting places of loved ones:
    family, relatives, and friends.
There are monuments for a moment's memory.
With names and dates of birth and death,
    they commemorate someone who was loved
    and is now mourned and missed.
They call to mind outstanding achievements
    of those who helped to make our world better.
Cemeteries remind us of eternity and tell us
    there is still time to serve you.
Good night, Lord.

Bright Side

Thinking back over this day,
    it's safe to say not everything went right.
Troubles, though, can be blessings
    when they lead to you, Lord.
Some people find their way back to you
    through crisis.
Some only cry out to you when they hit bottom.
Accidents, sickness, heartbreaks may be
    graces in disguise.
Teach me, Lord, to be on the lookout for some good
    from the disappointments in life,
    to see, perhaps, your footprint
    along a rocky road of failure.
Good night, Lord.

July 25

Hearing

How does a man feel who lived his life in silence
and one day with a hearing aid
hears the voice of a loved one?
What is it like to not hear,
and then one day to hear?
What a blessed moment, an occasion of grace!
Many of us, Lord, rediscover your greatness
when, with the help of your grace,
we really begin to hear you.
Grant that I may hear your voice
and never harden my heart to it.
You have communicated to me;
let me forever hold your word sacred.
Good night, Lord.

July 26

Rights

The struggle for equal rights, civil rights . . .
Lord, it seems it will never end,
what with protest marches and magazine articles.
If only we had the vision
to see one another as you created us.
Each person deserves equal treatment
because you have created us equal.
Each has an inherent dignity
that demands recognition and basic equality.
Inspire those with more to live more simply
so that all may simply live.
With our hearts free of prejudice,
all we have to do is love one another.
Good night, Lord.

Improvement

If the just person falls seven times a day,
    as your Good Book says, Lord,
    I guess I've made several culpable mistakes today.
What a challenge to improve on that.
If at first I do not succeed,
    I must try, try again.
Being human is no excuse to become
    used to failings and live comfortably with them.
Let me improve, Lord, a little bit each day.
It demands honest effort and a firm resolve
    to even want to sin less.
A heartfelt act of contrition goes a long way.
With your grace, strengthen my resolve.
Good night, Lord.

Lifestyles

Lifestyles of the wealthy and poor clash, Lord.
As this day wanes, my conscience nudges me.
Poverty and wealth dictate how human beings live.
There is sharp contrast between the poor and the rich.
It has been this way for centuries,
    but the reports are that this gap is growing.
"The poor you always have with you."
Vacationers cruise to foreign lands, exotic islands
    and they witness families ghettoed in poverty.
They return to their hotels and lounge at the poolside.
Are they pretending the destitute do not exist,
    that there is nothing that can be done for them?
Inspire us to improve conditions of the "other half."
Good night, Lord.

July 29

Anger

There are times, Lord, when for your sake
  I must become angry and express it.
But explosive anger is not a solution.
People losing control are like volcanoes
  spitting debris and causing destruction.
Bless me with patience and even controlled outrage
  when I witness injustice.
Let my love be patient and long-suffering.
Help me to remain cool under pressure,
  discovering release in humor, in jogging, in prayer.
When there is provocation, may my anger
  be expressed in reasonable ways.
Bless me with quiet confidence and an inner peace.
Good night, Lord.

July 30

Ecology

"Environmentally sensitive," Lord, describes
  those who respect your creation.
Mother Earth, delicately balanced, belongs to you,
  and you have entrusted it to us,
  a treasure borrowed from our grandchildren.
We are all responsible for the conservation
  of the fields and streams, lakes and woodlands.
How beautiful your majestic mountains, Lord,
  waterfalls and flowered meadows.
We see the work of your hands
  in the snowy-headed eagle and golden canary.
Grant that we may preserve this precious gift
  and realize that our welfare is tied to it.
Good night, Lord.

Close to You

There is nothing that is impossible
    if you are with me, Lord.
Without you, I am weak, unreliable,
    but together we can do what needs doing.
I do well to acknowledge my complete dependence
    on you, Lord, the source of all being and goodness.
Something may happen to throw me off balance,
    to induce anxiety—secret fears, perhaps.
Help me to regain composure,
    placing my hands in yours, Lord.
You are my wisdom and my strength.
I shall not fear if you are with me.
May your grace keep us ever close.
Good night, Lord.

August 1
Pursuit of Truth

Each day, Lord, like this one, is another leg
   in the journey of life to discover truth.
"What is truth?" Pilate asked sarcastically.
It's reality grasped by the mind,
   the conformity of the inside with the outside.
With more important and less important truths,
   may I learn the difference and order my priorities.
Acquiring truth is progressive and gained slowly,
   often through trial and error.
Complete truth is elusive and the pursuit goes on.
You, Lord, are the source of truth and total Truth;
   no one else possesses it entirely.
Let me find contentment knowing you, the Truth.
Good night, Lord.

August 2
Separation

The pain of separation defies logic, Lord.
Words cannot control the emotional swell
   that engulfs the human spirit.
It comes when sweethearts part,
   when children are snatched from their parents,
   when hostages are kidnapped,
   when death visits a home.
Sustain us, Lord, and give us strength
   at times of bitter separation.
When nothing seems to make sense at those times,
   help us to place ourselves blindly in your hands—
   and hold on tight with hope.
Good night, Lord.

Troubled Children

Bless our children, Lord;
   deliver them from confusion and turmoil.
Today's society is volatile, unpredictable, violent.
People switch loyalties, take detours,
   and go off in all directions, not always toward you.
I pray for those who are in one way or another
   caring for our impressionable children.
Let us have reason to hope, I pray.
Help us, Lord, to control our lives
   and to stabilize the lives of our young.
Let them learn of you from people of faith.
Their security rests in their parents, in their families,
   in their homes and schools—and especially in you.
Good night, Lord.

Broken Hearts

Lord, I was thinking today about people
   whose love relationship is troubled:
   spouses, the engaged, sweethearts.
They must want to sing the blues:
"There's a tear in my beer tonight."
Was it only infatuation, Lord,
   that led to these broken hearts?
Sweethearts search for each other, find each other,
   and tire of each other.
They "fall in love," and then fall out.
Let all those reeling from stormy relationships
   find comfort in you, and the wisdom
   to work toward a loving reconciliation.
Good night, Lord.

August 5
Remembering
Life is seen in better perspective, Lord,
    when we remember the wonderful people of the past.
We celebrate days of remembrance, memorial days,
    when we recall those who sacrificed their lives in wars,
    and those who served you especially well, your saints.
We recall those closer to us,
    those who have touched our lives,
    departed loved ones, our family and friends.
Thank you, Lord, for all these people,
    for all they have done for us.
Thank you for being present to us in them.
Continue to be with us, I pray,
    and may we always remember and praise you.
Good night, Lord.

August 6
Mixed Signals
There are mixed or broken signals about you, Lord.
Many people are confused or completely ignorant
    about religion, about you.
What is correct? What is true? How do we find God?
Confusion is not your fault, Lord;
    you are the perfect communicator.
Our reception may not be so good.
Are our lines open? Is there static on the line?
Are we tuned in to the right station?
Raise up prophets who can read the signs of the times,
    who can interpret your will accurately
    and summon us to holy deeds.
Then we may receive your word more clearly.
Good night, Lord.

Challenges

Challenges in the public and private arenas
    are not entirely new, are they, Lord?
News today consists of events like those that happened
    to different people at another time and place.
All of us, then and now, New Age or Middle Ages,
    share humanity's aspirations and inherent weaknesses.
Grant, Lord, that we not think we have all the answers
    and that our ancestors can teach us nothing.
Let us keep our minds and hearts open
    to what was right and what was wrong in the past
    so that we may learn to create a society
    after your own heart.
Bless us with wisdom and foresight.
Good night, Lord.

Stars and Stripes

I've become meditative tonight, Lord,
    because I was struck by the number of flags I saw today.
The flag should be more than a symbol—
    it should be an inspiration.
Old Glory represents us, the millions who make up
    "one nation, under God, indivisible,
    with liberty and justice for all."
It is a reminder to be active and work diligently
    to make liberty and justice become a reality.
Strengthen us as a nation, Lord, to cultivate
    a harmonious, caring atmosphere.
Justice and freedom go hand in hand.
Thanks for our country.
Good night, Lord.

August 9

Aging

Lord, as I move through life and get older,
    even after "retirement,"
    may I never turn my back on challenges.
A churchman said he'd rather burn out than rust out.
May all those who think they have done enough
    feel uncomfortable.
This is something you do not do, Lord:
    you never say you have done enough.
I understand why people need rest and recreation,
    but once refreshed and renewed, may they go on,
    seeking and meeting new challenges.
As age creeps up, I may have to change directions—
    but I pray that I may continue to serve you.
Good night, Lord.

August 10

It Can Be Done

My thoughts tonight, Lord, focus on men and women
    whose lives are real success stories.
They were deserving folks down on their luck
    who broke the vicious cycle of poverty
    and climbed out of its deep pit
    by sheer determination and hard work.
They conquered heavy discouragement
    and endured even the arrogant remarks
    of those who were "doing better."
They didn't think the world owed them a living.
I pray, Lord, for those others
    still imprisoned by negative thoughts.
Let me help them to help themselves.
Good night, Lord.

Just Married

How much joyful expectation, Lord,
  is in the hearts of newly-weds?
Bless them and help them in their life together.
May their happiness be sustained in the years to come.
Let their love mature and grow stronger
  with each new day.
Let them learn to share, Lord, to make wise decisions,
  and to comfort each other.
When children are born, may they be welcomed
  as blessings and as priceless opportunities
  to share their love even more.
May those recently united in hand and heart
  find courage and strength in you.
Good night, Lord.

No Place Like Home

Lord, may there be many happy homes in our land:
  in apartments, farmhouses, condominiums,
  split levels, and cottages by the sea.
Harmony is so elusive in many homes.
Home ought to be a haven of peace, a place of love.
Be it ever so humble, there is no place
  as meaningful as one's home.
It is where love is spoken, Lord,
  where there is consideration in conversation,
  where you are honored by honorable lives,
  where you are acknowledged openly—
  in prayer, in ritual, symbols, and deeds.
Inspire each family member to make home special.
Good night, Lord.

August 13
True Home
Our true home is with you, Lord—
  wherever we may live.
Some have lived in one house all their lives.
Others—military, sales reps, missionaries, scientists—
  have lived in homes all over the world.
Still others want to travel to discover new lands,
  see what's across the ocean or continent.
How challenging for those who long
  for lasting friendships and stable relationships.
Help us to remember, though,
  that you, Lord, are our destiny and are always with us.
Wherever we go,
  strengthen us on our journey.
Good night, Lord.

August 14
The Lighthearted
Blessed are the lighthearted, Lord,
  those who are pleasant to be around,
  and whose outlook is positive.
Each day we meet the serious-minded and the upbeat,
  and it's more fun with the cheerful.
Being lighthearted should be one of the beatitudes.
I can cultivate a carefree attitude
  if I focus on your loving presence, Lord.
The lighthearted have the same responsibilities
  as those with permanently wrinkled foreheads,
  but trust in your presence explains the difference.
Despite life's tough blows, may I
  always have the lightheartedness of your children.
Good night, Lord.

The Sorrowful
Comforting the sorrowful really does help, Lord.
We all know because we have been there.
Nighttime prayer is a wonderful opportunity
    to consider what is important in relationships,
        what works, and what does not.
Letting friends know we share their feelings
    is true comfort in an hour of need.
It is a work of mercy, a labor of love.
Soften my heart, Lord, when I encounter
    others shouldering heavy burdens.
Inspire me to hold their hands and lead in prayer.
You are the pillar of our strength.
There is no greater comfort than your loving arms.
Good night, Lord.

Great Expectations
Lord, for all your children,
    is there ever a day without some expectation?
We all need something to look forward to;
    they call it hope.
Children can't sleep on Christmas eve.
Young people look forward to the great day
    when they'll be grown up.
Exciting choices and challenges lie ahead.
May we all persevere in life's journey, Lord,
    with a steadfast spirit to please you.
And may our plans always include you.
We expect to be restless
    until we arrive at the end of life's rainbow.
Good night, Lord.

Joy of Living

I experience deep joy in living, Lord.
Living for 100 years would not exhaust my delight.
And, looking forward to being with you for eternity
    will not deplete my contentment.
You give me challenging opportunities to learn
    and many rewarding experiences.
Glorious sunsets are never precisely duplicated,
    and autumn leaves enflame my soul, Lord.
There are insights into personalities, too,
    finding generosity, gentleness, and grace.
There is no time for boredom;
    it is banished by your gift of a searching mind.
Thank you for this wonderful world.
Good night, Lord.

Faith

Faith is a powerful force, Lord,
    one of your many gifts.
It means believing in you;
    I mean, really believing,
    holding on to you, no matter what.
It means taking your word at face value.
Faith means hanging in there, even if there is no miracle.
Without it, Lord, I cannot please you.
Sometimes I say I believe, but I falter.
I pray that you strengthen my faith,
    that I may always be faithful to your word.
It is a bridge between heaven and earth,
    between you and me.
Good night, Lord.

Peace

What can I do about all this violence, Lord?
Doesn't peace have to be an active force,
    since passivity produces nothing?
As I pray tonight, I know it is wishful thinking
    that if I don't pay attention, the violence will go away.
Hatred erupts and people suffer.
People are engaged in wars in so many places;
    bombs are falling and snipers kill pedestrians.
Let there be peace on earth, Lord,
    and the needed justice as its foundation.
And I pray that I may be a peacemaker,
    ready to do what I can
      in personal matters or public policy.
Good night, Lord.

One Family

Lord, as I'm about to close this day,
    I'm convinced we are truly one family on earth.
Our pledge of allegiance should declare that we are
    "one family under God."
We need to think "family" much more than we do.
There is no "them" and "us,"
    just us.
This ideal way of seeing others is yet to be realized.
Do we ask the color of your skin, Lord?
May we all develop color blindness
    and see only family members.
There are no enemies, only brothers and sisters.
If we love you, we love one another. Period.
Good night, Lord.

Daily Blessings

For the simple things in life, thank you, Lord.
It's good to take nothing for granted
   and to appreciate everything.
Hospital patients, restricted from walking the hall
   or using the bathroom, come to appreciate the routine.
What I need is a keen sense of gratitude.
I acknowledge your generosity, Lord,
   in the sun that warms me, in rain that gives me drink.
May I see blessings in the thoughtfulness of friends,
   and the kindness of family members and strangers.
Let me not suddenly cherish what is at hand
   only with the threat of losing it.
With all my heart, I am grateful to you.
Good night, Lord.

Detours

Detours, Lord—many of us have turned off
   the charted courses that lead to you.
In pursuit of happiness,
   I travel roads that lead me away from you.
Satisfaction is sought in bottles or narcotics;
   raw pleasure is in the pornographic.
In blatant conflict of sacred marriage vows,
   infidelity is mistakenly billed
   as some sort of insider's paradise.
Lead us not into temptation, Lord.
Let there be no deceiving detours in my life.
Lead me back to you if I stray.
You are my Good Shepherd.
Good night, Lord.

Weather

How changeable the weather, Lord!
We accept it because we don't have mastery
    over the snow, the rain, the sun, and the wind.
Is the wind soundless?
It catches the trees, the windows, and other things
    like an eerie, foreboding voice.
The weather is part of our lives.
It can help us relate to you, Lord.
How marvelous the universe, your creation—
    your power, your command.
And how unmodified and steadfast your love,
    despite the unpredictable forces of nature!
You alone are my creator God.
Good night, Lord.

Starvation

Millions battle starvation each day, Lord.
This evening I am quite content after a good meal.
I dash to fast food restaurants for hamburgers,
    french fries, cole slaw, and the rest.
Sometimes I dine in slow food places, you know,
    cocktails, appetizers, salads, a variety of courses.
I think about my brothers and sisters, Lord,
    in barrios, in drought-stricken areas,
    strangled by famine—and it bothers me.
I feel guilty for not sharing more,
    for not being more active politically, for not praying.
Thanks for this sensitivity; it's a beginning.
The cause is close to your heart.
Good night, Lord.

Denial

It's strange, Lord, how sentences and phrases
    spring into my head, especially at night.
"Before the cock crows twice,
    you will deny me three times!"
This warning echoes through the centuries.
Peter was afraid, and so am I at times.
Let your grace assist me to surmount temptation
    and to make up for my weaknesses.
May I never deny the truth: about family, heritage,
    identity, and, most of all, my faith in you, Lord.
Give me the courage to be honest with myself
    and to respect everyone and judge no one.
Peter overcame his fear; grant me the same.
Good night, Lord.

Taken In

Taking advantage of someone's weakness or ignorance
    must be so distasteful to you, Lord.
Big children manipulate little ones.
Con artists fleece unsuspecting investors.
They say there's a sucker born every minute.
How many empty gold mines or swampland acres
    have glib and slippery sales reps sold?
People buy miracle creams for prolonged youth
    only to discover wrinkles when they wash.
It is a matter of naked dishonesty, Lord.
Help me not to be taken in—by phone or in person—
    swayed by greed for quick, unearned wealth.
Grant me the grace of prudence.
Good night, Lord.

Realistic Expectations

Evening prayer can be quite sobering, Lord.
Give me, I pray, realistic expectations.
We have all seen too many movies
    and been exposed to great fantasy and fiction.
We grow up on fairy tales, super characters,
    larger than life images on TV and in print.
Most people can discern the real and the unreal;
    still, some form notions of success
    far from down-to-earth achievements.
If I shoot for the stars, Lord,
    let me keep my feet on the ground, my eyes open.
In the final analysis, lasting happiness lies with you,
    only with you!
Good night, Lord.

Window of the Soul

Lord, as I'm about to close my eyes on this day,
    I think, what a great blessing they are.
They are the window to my soul.
Thank you for them
    and for all that they allow me to see.
They enable me to read, to admire landscapes,
    to recognize friends and family,
    to gaze into the eyes of my beloved.
Allow me, Lord, to use my eyes
    unto your praise and glory.
May what I decide to admit through this window
    lead me, at your pleasure,
    to the everlasting sight of you.
Good night, Lord.

August 29
Overconfidence

When I forget I'm completely dependent on you,
    Lord, that's overconfidence.
Humility is an equalizer and my protection.
What a hollow state of bravado
    when I believe I can stand on my own.
Independent I am not.
There is only one truly independent being, Lord,
    and it is you, Being itself.
I depend on you for my next breath,
    and for my very existence.
I enjoy perfect confidence
    when it rests unreservedly in you.
Thank you for your gift of life.
Good night, Lord.

August 30
Children

Bless the children, Lord.
I hope they're praying tonight and again at morn,
    offering their day to you.
Tomorrow they'll be getting ready for school,
    searching for socks and shirts,
    boarding their buses or walking down the street.
Parents will give last minute reminders,
    encouragement, and goodbye kisses and waves.
May their guardian angels watch over them.
May they be kind in the corridors and classrooms
    and on the playgrounds.
Help them to realize that their goal
    is to know and love you.
Good night, Lord.

Motives

There is power in the human will, Lord.
Folks can accomplish the extraordinary
    when their motives are strong and demanding enough.
Tiny women lift huge weights in emergencies;
    men endure dreadful hardships to live.
People exercise strength beyond capacity
    in the unique challenges they face.
How can they be so powerfully motivated?
Is it because they just wanted something so much?
You have to be at their side, Lord.
We must think positively, say it can be done.
Above all, let genuine love motivate our lives
    so that we may serve one another.
Good night, Lord.

September 1
Near Miss

There are many near misses in life, Lord.
I must come close to catastrophe more than I'm aware.
Shall I thank my guardian angel for this?
Once I jogged around a corner and off a curb,
    and I was almost struck by a car.
I made a quick check of my conscience.
There is no way to live except in your good graces.
There can be no cutting corners, Lord,
    when it comes to right or wrong.
There are no shortcuts to happiness.
Since I don't know the day or the hour
    when you will call me to account, let me be prepared.
Close calls are warning signals.
Good night, Lord.

September 2
Sharing Joy

It is good to rejoice in another's good fortune.
Lord, sharing joy is part of our own happiness.
There is reason to celebrate if a friend
    graduates with honors or lands an exciting job.
If a couple joins their hands and hearts in matrimony,
    let me be a member of those wishing them well.
A new baby is a blessed event,
    an event that gladdens everyone's heart.
Our congratulations add to the lucky person's delight.
There's no room for envy in generous souls.
Our appreciation of your blessings on others
    brings us closer to them and to you.
Thanks for all your favors, whoever gets them.
Good night, Lord.

Addiction

Sin is slavery, Lord, and we are all meant to be free.
My evening prayer begs you
to remove the shackles of the addicted.
Such habits hold the human spirit in a vise grip.
Gambling can consume funds and security;
too many are hooked by alcohol,
and narcotics hold them prisoner;
pornography insidiously grips the soul,
blocking out what is truly beautiful and good.
"Blessed are the pure of heart,
for they shall see God."
Lift the shades of blindness, Lord,
and let us behold your face in all we do.
Good night, Lord.

God's Perspective

Lord, a line from a time-honored hymn reminds us
how differently we see things:
"A thousand ages in your sight
are like an evening gone."
We lose sight of your perspective.
Some think of you, Lord, only in their own terms,
reducing you to human limitations and thought.
The world is too much for us to capture with a glance,
but not for you, Lord.
This fast-moving planet with jets and satellites,
love and pain, is hardly more than trivial to you.
You are awesome and beyond us,
except for your special love and presence.
Good night, Lord.

127

Happiness

What are we to say, Lord, if folks guage givers
    by the value of the gifts?
That's judging character by relying on expense.
Jewels from a rich person, they think,
    mean more than a flower from a child.
Midas was poor, despite his gold,
    and Jesus praised the widow for her penny.
We're in trouble if we think
    material things alone are of value.
Help us to view things religiously—from your angle.
Instill genuine values in us, Lord.
Contentment is largely a state of mind,
    and happy people see things your way.
Good night, Lord.

Lighting a Candle

No one is powerless, Lord, if they rely on you
    and work hard as if they are alone.
At the end of this day, with all its frustrations,
    I know you are attentive to our needs.
Many people feel ineffective in bettering the world,
    especially when it comes to objectionable media;
    they complain about the content of movies and TV.
Lord, bless these creative people
    who act, write scripts, operate cameras, and edit.
I pray that their efforts may be truly productive
    and that they may be guided by your will.
"Better to light one candle than curse the darkness."
May we never lose confidence in your aid.
Good night, Lord.

Good Self-Image

There is much talk, Lord, about the need
    to have a good self-image.
Some folks don't hold themselves in high esteem.
They feel inferior, less than their friends and neighbors.
We also have braggarts, arrogant people
    who are a "legend in their own mind,"
    who have an exaggerated idea of their importance.
Is this a cover-up for insecurity, a feint, braggadocio?
What we need is an honest picture of ourselves,
    a humble one, Lord.
Everyone is special and beautiful in your sight.
You have created us after your image.
If you are pleased with us as we are, all is well.
Good night, Lord.

Ecumenism

Lord, there are so many church communities
    professing belief in you and bearing your name,
    and they cannot be worshiping different gods.
Are they in competition, professing superiority?
Forgive us, Lord, for our limited vision.
No one can blame you for this confusion.
You are the one Lord of all.
Help us to grasp the meaning of "Our Father,"
    and bless our ecumenical efforts
    so that we may be one, as you have called us to be.
United we are strong, capable of meeting challenges.
Grant us insight into the causes of our fractured church.
Above all, let us love one another.
Good night, Lord.

Contrasts
As I pray to you tonight, Lord,
    I'm on an equal footing with everyone;
    in your sight we are all your children.
But we live in a world of contrasts
    where things are far from equal.
Good and evil are side by side,
    as well as wealth and poverty.
They are like wheat and weeds in the same field.
Some, like Dives, live in luxury,
    and are unmindful of the slum-dwellers
    who are swallowed up in squalor.
Help us to be caring and sharing,
    and to face the harsh realities of your children.
Good night, Lord.

Fool's Entertainment
"Crime is the entertainment of the fool."
Lord, seeing this line in the Book of Proverbs
    reminds me of the volumes of print about
    the evil we humans do to one another.
We have miles of film and videotape
    dramatizing violence and other crimes.
How sad, Lord, that so many of us
    find our entertainment in this.
Has all this desensitized and dehumanized us?
Is this just as inhumane as crowds cheering
    as wild beasts devour Christians in the Colosseum?
Purify us so that we may
    appreciate the good, the true, and the beautiful.
Good night, Lord.

Fear of the Lord

Tonight, Lord, in a moment of self-awareness
   I stand most humbly before you
   in reverence, admiration, and awe.
Is this the "fear of the Lord"
I read in the book of Proverbs?
I "fear" you, Lord, not because
   of what you can do to me
   (our usual meaning of "fear"),
   but because of who you are.
If someone insists on "fearing" you,
   let it take the form of deepest respect for you.
Let my peace of mind and security
   lie in your tremendous love for me.
Good night, Lord.

Unwed Mothers

How frightened and upset they must feel—
   teenagers who are unwed and pregnant!
Lord, there are many thousands
   of these young mothers with child.
They don't want to hear words of reprimand
   or lectures on misconduct.
Carrying human life,
   they now shoulder new responsibilities.
They face such important decisions:
   parenting, support, education, personal relationships.
Lord, bless them with courage and wisdom,
   and bless us with compassion and understanding.
There's never any excuse for us not to be loving.
Good night, Lord.

September 13

The Beautiful

Open my eyes and my ears, Lord,
    that I may appreciate the beauty about me:
    in people and sunrises, of course,
    but in worms and shoelaces too.
I am not praying to see beautiful things,
    but rather to see things as beautiful.
There is a difference.
Everything has its own beauty, doesn't it, Lord?
It's a matter of outlook and sensitivity.
Let me recognize you in the glory of creation—
    all creation.
I pray that I may take nothing for granted.
Let me wake up and smell the roses.
Good night, Lord.

September 14

The Bible

You communicate with us in many ways, Lord,
    in the sacred tradition of your church,
    in the lived holiness of your disciples, in nature,
    and in the word you speak in the holy Bible.
Grant that I may treasure these inspired writings.
Lord, let me be sensitive to your word
    as it has been handed down from ages past.
Let the Bible be my guide and comfort,
    my inspiration and source of prayer,
    your word to me today and every day.
Sensitive to your grace, may I embrace
    whatever it means for me
    as I seek you in the gritty details of life.
Good night, Lord.

Joy in Prayer

There is joy in praying to you, Lord.
As a child I had to be coaxed a bit to pray.
Church services seemed endless and uneventful.
But that was long ago.
I have since come to know you better.
There is peace and contentment, Lord,
    when all else is set aside for our conversation.
Sometimes I read inspiring books or the Scriptures,
    or recite the prayers once committed to memory,
    or let my being drink in your presence.
All forms of communication are good
    because I know you know how I feel.
You are my friend.
Good night, Lord.

Renewed Trust

Lord, it's just practical to depend on you,
    and unrealistic to depend on myself alone—
    to exclude you from the picture,
    as if I could do anything without you.
This is not an excuse for goofing off, Lord.
I'll still have to work
    as if everything does depend on me.
It's just wise to be realistic
    to know I am in your hands
    and can do nothing without you and your grace.
Am I not your child,
    skipping through life hand-in-hand with you?
Every day is an occasion for renewed trust.
Good night, Lord.

September 17

Falling Out of Love

People fall out of love, Lord.
It's sad, but it happens.
Divorce courts and broken homes bear witness to this.
Lovers fail, cheat, cut corners, become indifferent,
    cry, and are victimized.
"You don't bring me flowers any more."
Emotions become tangled and twisted,
    and there is darkness and depression.
My heart goes out to those in personal crisis,
    and I know yours does too.
Give them inner strength, I pray,
    and help them find a road to reconciliation.
You have enough love to sustain us all.
Good night, Lord.

September 18

Secret Fears

Lord, we all have secret fears to face.
I know I do, and you know that I do.
As I converse quietly with you tonight,
    you read my heart and know
    even my unexpressed, secret fears.
I can shield them from family and friends,
    but not from you, Lord.
Some of my fears are foolish;
    like shadows down an empty street,
    they dissolve with the sunlight.
They lurk ominously unless confronted.
With you at my side,
    I will try to face my fears.
Good night, Lord.

Nature's Homage

Lord, you've got the whole world in your hands.
The universe and all its wonders have come from you;
    your creative hand directs it from moment to moment.
You have mastery over all,
    from the Himalayas to the atom.
The hills, valleys, streams, canyons,
    and the wild blue yonder are yours, Lord.
I wonder if you are amused at human discovery,
    when we rocket off and orbit planets.
I also wonder how angry you must be
    by our rape, pillage, and despoliation of the world
    you entrusted to us.
All nature pays homage and gives you glory.
Good night, Lord.

Ownership

Most of us are quite clear about ownership, Lord.
If it's our home, car, or lawn equipment,
    other people must keep their hands off.
It's a matter of justice, we tell ourselves.
But it's funny, Lord, how flexible our convictions
    become dealing with other people's property.
How permissive we become taking things home
    from the motel, factory, or office—
    like pencils, nuts and bolts, towels, napkins—
    nickel and dime fringe benefits, we call them.
Help us, I pray, to temper our greed,
    our hunger for more and more things.
Let us be completely honest, and detached.
Good night, Lord.

Mature and Childlike
Lord, you told us to become like children.
Children teach us so much by their candor.
They are trusting, ready to believe and love;
    they are honest and humble.
All this wrapped up in a small package.
Children usually have it all together—
    until grown-ups slant their thinking.
Which is it, Lord?
I know that I'm to grow up and mature
    and also remain childlike.
It's not a matter of either/or.
By your grace, may I learn to be both;
    one includes the other.
Good night, Lord.

Decisions
I know, Lord, that it's just wishful thinking
    that I can please all the people all the time.
How nice—and unreal—not to have to take sides,
    to have it both ways.
But you have made it clear, Lord,
    that we can't serve you and the world at the same time.
All decisions carry a price tag.
But sometimes it's even hard to know
    which decision is the one for you.
Most of my quandaries are not dramatic:
    what to do at home, at work, or at school,
    but whatever they are, help me to view them
    from your perspective.
Good night, Lord.

Good Old Days

Lord, so many people long for the "good old days."
Nostalgia is in: music from another time,
    photos of days long gone by.
How is it that former times were better than these?
There's a lot of good in a return to "better days,"
    provided we don't begin to "live" back then,
    to escape from what needs doing here, today.
Addressing today's challenges is more realistic
    than looking over our shoulders.
Let us cherish good times,
    but let us see each new day as a fresh occasion
    to make our world a better place.
We must be forward-looking, for your sake.
Good night, Lord.

Terminal Illness

Terminal illness, Lord—
    will I ever have this diagnosis?
Thousands hear this jarring news each day.
How would I react?
I speculate a lot, Lord, just before retiring.
It's easier to do this now, when I'm in good health.
There may come a time when resignation to your will
    is the only sensible option.
What else can the afflicted do meritoriously
    except to offer their suffering to you?
I reflect on Calvary and your suffering
    and I pray for strength.
You are close and your love sustains me.
Good night, Lord.

Good Shepherd

"The Lord is my shepherd."
City folk who have never seen real sheep
    cherish this psalm;
        everyone does.
It declares that there is nothing we shall want,
    that you will care for our every need,
        that you will be with us when we need you.
And almost none of us have ever seen a shepherd.
We know, though, that you, Lord,
    are our caring, loving Shepherd
    with total devotion and loyalty to your flock.
It's such a comfort to know how solicitous you are.
We, the flock of your people, trust you.
Good night, Lord.

Praise in Pain

Lord, sometimes we experience pain
    that refuses to go away and gnaws at us:
        toothaches, headaches, backaches, arthritis.
Medication may be ineffective or unavailable.
Hot water bottles, ice packs, and aspirins
    don't bring comfort.
We groan, mumble, complain, and even pray.
There are even wild promises about life reform
    if relief ever comes.
I don't wish this on anyone.
Help me to place my hand in yours at such times
    and try to see some value in the experience.
If any of it is for your glory, then it's all right with me.
Good night, Lord.

Gratitude

We are admonished to pray with thanks, Lord.
Our petitions to you should come from a heart
    resigned to your will and filled with gratitude.
May our gratitude be for all we have,
    important or not, seen or not,
    even the commonplace and seemingly insignificant,
    but most especially for life itself.
You, Lord, are an artist turning out masterpieces,
    each different and perfect in its own way.
We are fashioned after your image,
    with intellect and free will and hearts for love.
We are overwhelmed with your precious gift of life.
Thank you.
Good night, Lord.

The Handicapped

We have become more conscious of
    and sensitive to the handicapped, Lord.
Bless those who are emotionally, mentally,
    and physically impaired.
Bless the work, also, of those who work
    for and with the disadvantaged.
We praise and encourage those who work for this cause.
There is always more for them to do:
    cures, alleviation of pain, access to public buildings.
Their goal and ours is to assist the handicapped
    to become self-reliant and self-sufficient.
All have dignity and are worthy of our respect.
Fill us with compassion.
Good night, Lord.

Faith Testimony

Give courage, Lord, to those who waver in their faith.
Nighttime seems to be the occasion
  when doubts of faith surface in every heart.
Stabilize those who are not quite sure
  of their relationship with you.
Help believers give witness to their faith.
Their testimony may strengthen the fainthearted.
A cancer victim praises your holy name.
A father and mother lose a child in death
  but demonstrate resignation to your will.
Alcohol and drug addicts succeed with an interior force:
  their faith and trust in you.
We believe, but help our unbelief.
Good night, Lord.

Making Time

Lord, help me to make time for what is important,
  to set priorities and strive after them.
As I review my day, I know only too well
  how crowded each day can become.
Being "too busy" suffocates thoughtfulness and sharing.
Families suffer, husbands and wives grow apart,
  and children are neglected.
Runaway ambition strangles loving relationships,
  and selfishness takes many forms.
Lord, my orientation is on the right track
  when centered on you.
Help me to seek first your kingdom;
  then all other matters will fall into place.
Good night, Lord.

Wisdom

You, Lord, are the source of all wisdom.
Let me not live the next day and the next year
   without the insight and sense
   that can come only from you.
Instead of the "wisdom" of the world,
   I pray, Lord, that I might live each day
   guided by the singlemindedness
   of one of your disciples.
Not to make you and your teaching
   a part of my decision making
   is like trying to run this world without its designer.
Open my mind to the wisdom
   that this world calls foolishness.
Good night, Lord.

Countdown

There is a season for everything, Lord,
   a time and a place to be born, to live, and to die.
This is not startling news in itself,
   but it can be if I make it very personal.
The countdown to the end of my life has begun.
Lord, is this a special blessing, a grace,
   a signal to get my life in order?
It is an opportunity to confront my sinfulness,
   recognize my sins, and to make amends.
I wonder sometimes about meeting you face to face.
How good it will be to have cultivated
   our friendship over the years!
Thank you for the grace of realizing this.
Good night, Lord.

October 3

Hospitality

Old world hospitality, Lord,
  is really divine hospitality;
    it's what you've always wanted from us.
Those who appear on the doorstep are welcomed.
A guest comes; you come.
A stranger comes; you come.
Visitors come, and it is you I welcome, Lord.
Let me not look far and wide to extend courtesy,
  but to do it to all who come to me.
Charity begins at home,
  that is, it begins at my doorstep;
    it continues with a glass of water given in your name.
My home is their home and your home.
Good night, Lord.

October 4

Praise the Lord

Lord, how good it is to praise you!
This is why we exist.
Let our praise not be limited to evening prayer,
  but extend to every moment of our existence.
Let us praise you, Lord, not with words alone,
  but with our minds, our lives, and all our actions,
    every day of our lives.
People used to greet one another on the street
  by saying "Praise the Lord!"
It is fitting that we give you praise and glory,
  that we recognize you and honor your presence
    in good times and in bad.
Praise to you, now and forever!
Good night, Lord.

Inspiration

How can I explain the origin of my thoughts, Lord?
Even at prayer, I wonder where they come from.
I even write them down and read them aloud,
    wondering about their source.
They can't have originated from me alone, I think.
Does this happen to journalists and poets?
When they read their own compositions,
    are they surprised and exclaim, "Did I write that?"
How wonderfully, Lord, you have fashioned
    our minds, spirits, emotions!
How exquisitely you inspire us
    to fill this world with beauty.
Let no one claim for self what is a gift from you.
Good night, Lord.

Refugees

The plight of refugees is in the news again, Lord.
It appears that we go from crisis to crisis,
    from country to country, continent to continent—
    people uprooted and fleeing disaster.
The story of these hapless, homeless people
    is all too common.
The poor we shall always have with us,
    but is this what you meant, Lord?
Thousands of people spilling over borders,
    fleeing revolutionaries, or escaping famine?
May they always be in our sight
    because out of sight means out of mind.
Make us sensitive to these, our brothers and sisters.
Good night, Lord.

October 7
Love
Lord, your wish is that we should love one another.
For all our efforts at communication,
   it may be that we still don't get the message.
Violence, rejection, oppression, broken homes—
   all suggest that we're still missing the point.
With radio, TV, satellite links, computers, and phones—
   all meant to bring us together—
   why, Lord, are we so often quite apart?
Help us to experience an interior transformation,
   a conversion in each of us and all of us,
   a cultivation of harmonious relationships
   with you and among ourselves.
Our prayer is that you bring us together.
Good night, Lord.

October 8
Solutions
When my friend and I talk over world problems, Lord,
   foreign aid, immigration, hunger, the death penalty—
   we have solutions for them all.
Too bad our officials don't take our advice, we joke.
But serious challenges threaten
   your kingdom of justice, love, and peace, Lord.
Injustice, hatred and violence aren't far from us.
Help us to do more than be informed, and to gripe,
   but to work for lasting solutions.
I'm afraid to think that if we're not part of the solution,
   we're part of the problem.
Bless those who put their lives or lifestyles at risk
   in order to improve this world.
Good night, Lord.

Daily Praise

The day is done, Lord,
    and I pray that I have given you glory today.
Every person every day has the opportunity
    to praise and glorify your holy name.
In sickness and in health, on good days and bad
    we can offer our lives as a prayer:
    as airline personnel pressured by anxious travelers,
    as commuters battling traffic,
    as umpires jeered by hometown fans,
    as researchers frustrated by missing documents.
We praise you by the sincerity of our lives.
For the privilege of serving and praising you,
I thank you with all my heart.
Good night, Lord.

Shut-Ins

Lord, some patients are so inspiring.
As I recount my blessings at evening prayer,
    I question my ability to cope in similar circumstances.
I suspect I might be plunged into deep despair.
But you provide grace to fit the challenge,
    don't you, Lord?
A diamond does not sparkle until it is cut.
Those who are shut-ins, homebound, limited in freedom,
    astound us with their liberated spirits.
Perhaps they know they hold
    a special place in your heart.
It is a privilege to visit them, who give us courage.
Their infirmity is an investment toward salvation.
Good night, Lord.

October 11

Quiet Prayer

There are times, Lord, when my mind goes blank.
This is the end of the day
    and I have nothing special to say to you.
It happens between friends, between spouses.
Perhaps they are all talked out, or just tired.
When speaking with you,
    there is no call for nervous spontaneity,
    compulsive talk to keep our conversation going.
My heart, sluggish for the moment, longs for you, Lord.
Maybe it is good merely to contemplate your goodness,
    to feel the assurance of your presence,
    to be still so that your grace may reach me.
Expression fails, but devotion perseveres.
Good night, Lord.

October 12

Quiet Time

It is good for the soul, Lord, to retreat and to rest.
For many busy people, the evening is a time to relax.
How important, how necessary it is
    to recharge our batteries,
    to renew and refresh ourselves,
    so that we can confront
    the next day's responsibilities, such as
    chauffeuring children to rehearsal and Little League.
Help me to use this quiet time
    to get in touch with myself and with you
    and enjoy the moment's tranquility.
I often see quite clearly
    when I close my eyes and listen.
Good night, Lord.

New Ideas

Lord, let me not become too set in my ways
 and be an obstacle to progress.
A static mind is so unrealistic and stifling
 because life—in all its aspects—is on the move.
I live in a developing world, Lord,
 where nothing stands still.
If I move away and later return
 to the old neighborhood, it's not the same.
I can't go back in time—it's a losing battle—
 except for a moment's memory.
Help me to be open-minded, open to new ideas,
 eager to engage in an ongoing world.
The life you give me is vibrant and meant to be that way.
Good night, Lord.

Heaven

Those who look beyond this world, Lord,
 have a greater grasp on the meaning of life.
We need our thoughts fixed on the eternal
 in order to keep them firmly on this life's affairs.
Many people limit their concerns to their present world:
 work, family, education, health.
To those who wonder "Is this all there is?"
 you, Lord, reveal what is beyond.
There is a greater perspective than the here and now.
It is everlasting life in a place called heaven,
 not a not dim and distant "pie in the sky,"
 but unending life with you.
May destiny—our destination—flavor our lives.
Good night, Lord.

October 15
God of Love

Lord, you are the God of love.
I dare not think of you
    as less than an all-loving, ever-present Father.
Nothing can contain you or know you fully,
    but I know that you love me!
As I pray to you this evening,
    that is how I think of you.
You created this world—and me—
    from nothing,
    simply because you wanted to share your life.
Yet you have given me the capacity to love,
    and I find fulfillment only in you.
I love you with the fullness of my being.
Good night, Lord.

October 16
Rain

I'm afraid, Lord, that we gripe about rain
    a lot more than we thank and praise you for it.
Rain alters our plans to go on picnics,
    but makes the corn, wheat, and flowers grow.
Rain gathers in lakes and rivers,
    providing a home for the fish we eat,
    but in its abundance floods our cities and fields.
Despite floods and droughts, Lord,
    you provide the rain that we need to live.
Like grace, it is often a blessing in disguise.
The next time it rains
    let me remember it as a gift
    and be grateful for it.
Good night, Lord.

Betrayal

One of the saddest scenes in scripture, Lord,
    is about betrayal by a kiss for thirty pieces of silver.
A kiss, a sign of love and respect,
    is used to betray another,
    throwing loyalty to the wind,
    turning its meaning upside down.
We deeply value it in our relationships:
    to individuals, organizations, our country.
As I pray this evening, Lord,
    strengthen me in my weakness.
Let my loyalty to those I owe it
    be secure, my allegiance steadfast.
My loyalty to them is a prime sign of my love.
Good night, Lord.

Judging

A person is to be presumed innocent, Lord.
Folks may assume the worst, make snap judgments,
    or fail to give the accused a break.
I pray this evening to be fair and patient,
    and not jump to conclusions
    or be judgmental in any way.
Anyone can accuse a person of anything,
    but basing it on evidence is something else.
Inspire us, Lord, to give all people
    the benefit of the doubt;
    let our minds and hearts be open to the truth.
We pray for openness and understanding.
You see us as no one sees us.
Good night, Lord.

October 19
Trusting God
As I was growing up, Lord, I was taught:
"Entrust your cares to God,
and God will support you."
As I close down the day, I realize
there is no other way to get through this life.
A childlike abandon to you will bring peace.
When I'm worried or troubled,
anxiety gnawing away at me,
I have to rely on your love and strength, Lord,
if I am to be balanced and sane.
There has to be a "letting go" of my burdens
from my shoulders to yours.
Watch over me and all will be well.
Good night, Lord.

October 20
My Security
I have heard wonderful stories
about people persevering under great hardship.
Lord, how slow I am to grasp simple truths.
But often with evening prayer you enlighten me.
What's the point of my life if I don't trust you?
Castles may crumble and dream worlds collapse,
but you always love me with a tremendous love.
Those who suffer realize their trials are not in vain
because you are with them.
In good times and in bad, Lord, you sustain me;
you are my comfort and security.
Your loving way is sometimes incomprehensible,
but unquestionably true.
Good night, Lord.

Love in Deed

I know, Lord, that you want me
    to put my money where my mouth is.
I am bothered by St. John's penetrating question:
    ". . . how can God's love survive in a someone
    who has enough of this world's goods
    yet closes his heart to his brother or sister in need?"
I admit, my conscience is nudging me.
It is difficult, Lord, to reconcile my gourmet meals,
    expensive clothing, and fashionable home
    with the poverty in the neighborhood and city.
Inspire me to love and to share freely,
    and not be choked by what I possess.
Help me to love in deed and not only in words.
Good night, Lord.

Possessions

Naked I came into this world and naked I shall leave it.
Job had it right, Lord.
Many—myself included—become afflicted with a fever
    to pile up possessions,
    consumed with a desire to accumulate.
At heart, we know we cannot take it with us,
    but we remain inordinately attached.
How sad, Lord, the scrambling, bickering, dickering,
    stabbing, and grabbing to acquire wealth.
How sad that we confuse "want" and "need."
Help me to learn that contentment
    does not depend on numbers or volume,
    but on our relationship with you and with others.
Good night, Lord.

October 23
Seeking Truth
When I was a child, Lord,
    my teacher wanted us to raise our hands
    if we failed to understand something.
School is over now, but I'm still raising my hand.
There is so much I don't understand—
    about you, about others, about this world.
Only you, Lord, know all things.
Continue to fill me with a desire for knowledge,
    and with the perseverance to pursue it,
    wherever it may be found.
Let me not fear anything I learn,
    for real knowledge can lead only to you.
Bless all in the pursuit of knowledge.
Good night, Lord.

October 24
Curiosity
Lord, you have instilled us with ceaseless curiosity.
As children, we asked our parents, teachers, friends
    "why?" a thousand times in our search for answers.
How many newspapers and magazines
    have I read over the years, how many hours of TV?
We even indulge in the gossipy kind.
Didn't you fill us with curiosity, Lord,
    as incentive to pursue happiness, union with you?
We even seem to be curious about curiosity.
How productive it can be
    when my curiosity is disciplined and channeled,
    leading to useful knowledge and to enjoyment.
I pray I may use it to find you.
Good night, Lord.

Nighthawks

There are nights, Lord, when sleep doesn't come easily.
Those who have a problem sleeping—nighthawks—
    do well to find comfort and ease in prayer at that time.
There is an old joke about cheaper rates at night.
Some find difficulty unwinding;
    they are worried and their motors keep running.
Some listen to talk shows, or watch seasoned movies.
Reading helps, and some turn to the Bible
    to encounter your word at a quiet moment.
You use many ways to touch us and guide us.
Grant that we may make good use of the opportunity.
May our hearts be receptive to your grace
    at any time of the day—or night.
Good night, Lord.

Feeling Helpless

What do I do, Lord,
    when I know something is wrong
    and can't do anything about it?
How powerless and helpless I feel.
Someone we love is drinking herself into the grave.
A co-worker is dipping his hand into the cash register.
The situation may call for diplomacy or tough love,
    but helping in some way can be very hard.
Sometimes, Lord, the other resents the intrusion
    and just stonewalls.
Help me at least to pray devoutly
    and remain steadfastly concerned for them,
    confident that your concern is far greater than mine.
Good night, Lord.

October 27

Taking the Time

Tonight, Lord, as my thoughts turn heavenward,
   I think, for some reason, of all the satellites in space.
Not many years ago there were none,
   and today many of them circle the planet.
It struck me that that capability was always available.
It was simply a matter of discovery, gradual learning,
   accumulated expertise, and scientific findings
   passed from generation to generation.
Telephone, radio, television, computers—
   all were possible in every century.
All knowledge, all progress is known to you at a glance,
   but for us some things just take time.
Help me to know what this means for me and the world.
Good night, Lord.

October 28

Parents

Parents are the most influential people in the world.
Collectively, Lord, they have a greater impact
   than a mountain of public relations firms.
Their children's journeys toward maturity
   are experiences of human enrichment.
While there are abilities and individual characteristics,
   parents help to form their children's
   attitudes, values, and perspectives.
What a great trust you place in their hands, Lord!
They have your grace and blessings in their mission
   to lead their offspring to you and to teach them
   to serve their brothers and sisters in the world.
Help them to communicate that you are Our Father.
Good night, Lord.

Discipline

"The Lord disciplines you,
    even as a father disciplines his son."
This is your word, Lord, echoing through the centuries.
It's a big mistake not to correct or admonish
    those we love and are responsible for.
Teachers do this and so do parents;
    they love their children and want what is best for them.
Lord, some people attribute their misfortune to you,
    as if it came upon them through some whim of yours.
They forget that you chastise those you love.
Grown-ups, in time, come to thank their parents
    for their loving discipline over the years.
Let us never forget: you are our loving Father.
Good night, Lord.

Loving Person

This is my thought, Lord, as I review the day.
You challenge us, Lord, to be loving persons;
    you call us individually to such a life.
Our maturity is ultimately gauged by our relationship
    of love with you and those around us.
Let me not, Lord, measure my success
    by degrees, awards, possessions, or influence.
I may be honored if folks erect a statue of me
    but if I fail in love, I am a hollow, useless being.
Can I live by and for down-to-earth love?
You do not ask the impossible.
Day by day, I can advance in holiness.
You are my strength and my motive.
Good night, Lord.

October 31

Waste Not

Some of us are fussy eaters, Lord.

I wonder sometimes if we are born or made that way.

We pick, and choose, and even leave food on our plates
     because we don't like the taste.

This can't be avoided entirely, but can there be less of it?

Perhaps when very young we became sick
     because of certain foods or were allergic to them.

In some cities, folks collect perfectly good leftovers
     from restaurants and bring them to soup kitchens.

That is the attitude I pray for, Lord.

May I never neglect to thank you for food and drink.

There are too many brothers and sisters less fortunate.

Let me always appreciate that you sustain us.

Good night, Lord.

Giving and Receiving

Lord, we long for time off,
    and then don't know what to do with the time.
Carefree days, with time on our hands,
    are often are boring and make us restless.
Are we too work-oriented?
Hours grind away slowly when we aren't goal-oriented.
Help me, Lord, to be more mindful of others
    when I have some time to spare.
There are letters to write, shut-ins to cheer,
    projects to do, and errands to run.
Somebody, somewhere, needs me.
It's the only way to give you glory.
It is in giving that we receive.
Good night, Lord.

Talking Over Problems

It's helpful, Lord, to discuss my problems with someone.
How do I solve domestic disputes,
    complications at the office?
Talking gives me a handle on the challenge
    and sheds light on possible solutions.
I should find a patient, prudent person
    and bring the bothersome issue to the surface.
Aside from others,
    there's always you I can turn to.
My evening prayer provides an opportunity
to talk things over with you, Lord.
No one but you knows all the answers.
Guide me so that I may always do your will.
Good night, Lord.

November 3

Character Formation

As you formed me, Lord, out of love,
    let me work at forming my character
    out of love for you.
Good habits form good character.
"Sow an act and you reap a habit,
    sow a habit and you reap a character,
    sow a character and you reap a destiny."
Lord, let this be my rule of thumb every day,
    something that springs from my love for you:
    in the way I speak to and about others,
    in the way I do my work at home and on the job,
    in the way I share my goods with those who need them.
Let my life be integrated and cultivated with your love.
Good night, Lord.

November 4

Unappreciated Love

Help me, Lord, not to be angry or discouraged
    if someone doesn't respond to my acts of love
    or acknowledge them.
My love is not to be conditioned on the reaction to it,
    on whether the other is grateful or not.
This is a lesson I learn from you, Lord.
Despite our rejection or underappreciation of your love,
    you look upon us with a never-failing love.
Help me to love others in deed
    because it's the right thing to do,
    not because I'll be thanked or rewarded.
If I love for what I get out of it,
    it's just love of myself, isn't it?
Good night, Lord.

Divine Friendship

A cheerful greeting is in order tonight, Lord,
  because of our relationship,
    not because it was a particularly good day for me
    or because I'm in a good mood for some reason.
As I prepare to end this day,
  I think of the union we share
  and it overwhelms and humbles me.
Our relationship is all that really matters, Lord.
Our conversation tonight is between friends,
  not just between creator and creature.
Just to be with you is more than I deserve.
Thank you for the unspeakable honor
  of being your child and friend.
Good night, Lord.

False Gods

"You shall not have false gods . . ."
Lord, that is your command.
I wonder how applicable it is.
I don't worship idols, do I?
To worship anyone or anything but you, Lord,
  is a terrible mistake.
Let me not bow in adoration to money or talents I have,
  to positions of power and influence,
  to drugs or alcohol,
  or to self-centeredness, worshiping myself.
Everything is far less than you.
There is no honest priority
  unless you are first in my life.
Good night, Lord.

November 7

The Lord's Name

You command us, Lord, not to use your name "in vain."
Your holy name is above all other names
    and it is to be uttered with reverence.
To defile your name is to defile you.
To speak your name in jest, in curse, in slang,
    or as witness to a false statement is to show disrespect.
We bow our heads at your name, Lord.
How painfully offensive it is
    to hear your holy name abused!
Those who try to be macho by speaking it irreverently
    defile what is sacred.
It is you we honor
    by speaking your name with reverence and awe.
Good night, Lord.

November 8

The Lord's Day

Your voice, Lord, echoes through the chambers of time:
    "Remember to keep the Lord's Day holy"—
    a day dedicated to you in a special way.
Your commandment is valid for all times.
May we never lose sight of it in our busy lives.
We are to set aside the one day
    for worshiping you as a family, a community.
This is your desire for your people, Lord.
Six days are fine for earning our daily bread,
    but Sunday is to be kept holy by everyone.
Some may think Sunday is just another day,
    but it is a special expression of our esteem for you.
Blessed are you and blessed is your command.
Good night, Lord.

Sex

There are such opposing views
    when it comes to your gift of sex, Lord.
Some would justify their immoral behavior
    by saying it's all right
    when it's between consenting adults.
Since when, I have to wonder,
    did consent become a norm for right and wrong?
There is so much confusion, Lord, about how
    we should use the freedom you have given us.
Let me see my freedom as the right to do as I ought,
    not as I please.
I pray that in sexual matters
    I may appreciate your gift and follow your holy law.
Good night, Lord.

Theft

You have commanded us, Lord, not to steal,
    to walk in justice with our sisters and brothers,
    giving to everyone what is due to them.
Living this way benefits everyone, including myself.
The threat of thievery propels us to protect our property;
    we have to spend money on locks, safes,
    security systems, alarms, police, and prisons.
Grant, Lord, that I may be honest in every respect.
Is there some way I steal from others:
    small items from the workplace or a store?
    someone's reputation by an imprudent word?
Help me to respect others' possessions,
    living together in a society that honors you.
Good night, Lord.

Purifying Intentions

It's time to close up shop for the day, Lord,
  to pray that my heart is in the right place—
  or ask forgiveness if it isn't.
It is called purifying my intentions.
If I should sin, the deed was first conceived within.
Temptations are only attractions to sin;
  they can be overcome, Lord, with your grace.
May my intentions always be to please you,
  and when I want something more than you,
  purify them, I pray.
Let me not cater to desires that lead me from you.
This is clear advice for peaceful living,
  and a peaceful conscience is your blessing.
Good night, Lord.

November 12
Cheerleader

Cheerleaders are organized to provide encouragement,
  and that is what we need from you, Lord.
Who does not need some form of cheerleading?
Every day we need your support and motivation
  to prop us up and enflame our hearts.
Cheerleaders chant and bounce around,
  synchronize formations, and create choreography.
Crowds are stirred, emotions soar,
  and, presumably, the team tries harder.
Prayer and quiet, thoughtful moments
  allow you a moment to act as our cheerleader.
We must never forget your loving presence;
  that is what encourages us most.
Good night, Lord.

Unwanted Music

Explicitly sexy or violent songs are proclaimed
    over the airways and heard by thousands—
    and you hear them too, Lord.
Composers and lyricists may feel daring and defiant.
(In Genesis, Adam and Eve suffered for like sentiments.)
This exploitation may sell music, Lord,
    but it preys upon human weakness
    and may be the occasion of sin and discontent.
We all benefit from moral restraint, good order,
    and respect for your laws.
With your grace, I will never consider
    another way of life that leads to self-destruction.
Thanks for your eminently practical commandments.
Good night, Lord.

Loving the "Unlovable"

Lord, you never said it would be easy.
No one is excused from loving those who are difficult.
Who can persevere in loving the "unlovable"?
In loving when the love isn't returned?
Mothers and fathers do when it comes to their children.
Husbands and wives, too,
    if they are giving and faith-filled.
As I seek reconciliation in this nighttime prayer,
    I can see that you are truly great-souled.
Your love us despite our lack of cooperation;
    your love continues even when we reject it.
Gather to yourself those that others may find unlovable.
May our hearts be open to your unending love.
Good night, Lord.

Time

I have to remind myself, Lord,
  that I could live better if I got a better handle on time.
Some pursue power and wealth
  as if there were no tomorrow.
If time is the measure of motion,
  I pray that my use of the time you give me
  will move me closer and closer to you.
They say we only go around once.
In that case, how profitable it would be for me
  to store up treasure in heaven,
  to live each moment for your praise and honor.
There is no such thing as wasted time
  if I am intent on doing your holy will.
Good night, Lord.

Death

I ask you, Lord, that I may see death—my death—
  as my birth to new life with you.
Death is not life's greatest finality,
  but life's quiet entrance to the banquet you promised.
The sorrow and separation that death brings
  are only part of the picture.
Let me look upon death this way, Lord,
  hope-filled and confident of your eternal presence.
Can I embrace it and not fear it?
Can I look it in the face and ask,
  "Death, where is your sting?"
I have your word that I can.
This is enough for me.
Good night, Lord.

Religious Convictions

I wonder, Lord, do you smile
    at our different images of you?
    at our different ways of worshiping you?
Do they all lead to you?
You can't be happy when we quarrel or persecute
    or criticize or act superior to those
    who seek you sincerely, as best they can.
Grant us, Lord, the grace to respect
    the religious convictions of everyone.
We pray that we all may be one in you.
How important it is to teach this to our children.
Open our minds and hearts to your truth,
    and let us all love you with our entire being.
Good night, Lord.

The Law of the Lord

"Happy the one who follows not the counsel
    of the wicked, but delights in the law of the Lord."
May these words of the psalmist speak to my heart;
    help me to memorize them and make them my own.
I want to embrace them as I would my own life.
I know, Lord, the "counsel of the wicked"
    can be pretty clever and luring.
The devil whispers that happiness is found in sin,
    but Satan is the great deceiver.
Clearly, happiness is not getting away with things.
You have a different set of directions.
Give me the wisdom to trust your way,
    to recognize that happiness is found in doing your will.
Good night, Lord.

November 19

Atoning for Sin

There's a lot of denial going around, Lord,
    when it comes to sin.
We don't have a real grasp on reality
    if we deny that there is such a thing.
Let me state it flat out:
    I am a sinner.
I am sorry for this, Lord, and I ask your forgiveness.
More than that, I want to atone for my sins.
If love makes up for a multitude of sins,
    let me live in love of you and all people.
Love reverses gears, changing selfishness to selflessness.
Generous deeds, love in action help to right the wrongs.
I thank you that I can atone for my sins.
Good night, Lord.

November 20

Obedience

All of us, Lord, like Moses,
    have to do "exactly what the Lord commanded."
Considering the hardship this would entail
    and the severe strain on his faith in you,
    this spiritual leader's obedience is remarkable.
How sweet it is, Lord, when someone
    does exactly what you want them to do!
Your ways, Lord, always work out for the best—
    in the long run.
And that's the problem: looking past the hardship that
    may be involved in seeing things through your eyes,
    being countercultural and willing to pay the price.
I pray you, give me this insight.
Good night, Lord.

Moods

Lord, you see our feelings changing from day to day,
　　like parents observing the moods of their children.
It shows we're made of flesh and blood, not stone.
This time of prayer gives me a chance
　　to reflect on my moodiness,
　　to lay the matter at your feet, Lord.
It's easy to smile when the sun is shining,
　　but when lowering clouds descend on me,
I know the sun is still shining behind them.
Lord, how do I keep an even keel in stormy weather?
I need a good boat to keep me afloat,
　　firm convictions, a foundation of faith,
　　and your grace—like a lighthouse—to guide me.
Good night, Lord.

Everybody's Doing It

"Everybody's doing it!" is a popular cop-out, Lord,
　　a justification for doing what's sinful.
Justifying misdeeds apparently was common practice
　　even in ancient times, as Exodus tells us:
　　"Neither shall you allege the example of many
　　as an excuse for doing wrong."
Peer pressure is strong, but, I pray, Lord,
　　that you give us strength to go against what's "in."
Grant me the grace to be a person of conviction,
　　to be steadfast without compromise.
To you alone do I owe loyalty.
Help those of us who have succumbed in weakness
　　to turn back to you.
Good night, Lord.

November 23
Rejoicing in the Lord
Jeremiah, your prophet, tells us not to be saddened,
   "for rejoicing in the Lord must be your strength."
How often do I get up in the morning thinking,
"There will be no sadness today
   because I am rejoicing in the Lord"?
We rejoice in so many other things;
   whoever says, "Let's party for the Lord"?
Tonight I thank you for realizing
   how much I should truly rejoice in you—
   not because of what you give me—
   but because you are always with me.
You yourself are my reason for rejoicing.
This thought has seldom crossed my mind—until now.
Good night, Lord.

November 24
Peaceful Sleep
I'm looking forward to a good night's sleep.
Lord, how good it is to slip peacefully into slumber.
How blessed are the little children
   who close their eyes and drift away
   almost anywhere and in any position.
Let me be relaxed and secure
   in the knowledge that you, Lord, are with me
   and that my cares matter to you.
There is nothing like quiet prayer in your presence
   to end the day,
   realigning my soul with you.
Into your hands
   I commend my cares and my spirit.
Good night, Lord.

God's Love

"I love you" can be said in countless different ways.
Lord, there must be a million songs
    that rephrase those three little words.
The Bible, your own word, shows us
    the different ways you tell us of your love:
    in creation, in the manna in the desert,
    in the inspired Israelite leaders,
    in your invitation to call you Father;
    in the Eucharist and in the resurrection—
    all are acts that shout your love for us.
You have begotten us, blessed us with life.
How shall I love you in return?
There is no one who is perfectly lovable, but you.
Good night, Lord.

Light for My Path

Lord, your word is a light for my path.
You are the way, the truth, and the life.
I welcome your guiding light
    when the night is dark,
    when the path is difficult and uncertain,
    when the crowd takes another route
    and jeers me for taking the less traveled path.
A person of faith, familiar with your word, Lord,
    knows how to find her way despite the obstacles.
Grant that I may become more familiar with your word.
You are not silent, but speak to me in many ways,
    in times past and present.
Your words are for all times, all seasons, all peoples.
Good night, Lord.

November 27

Possessions

Lord, your holy book tells us,
   "The just person's few possessions are better
   than the wicked person's wealth."
I pray for the courage and principle
   that all that I ever possess may be justly mine.
Those who shave accounts and deal under the table,
   those who pay substandard wages,
   those who steal from their employers
   will not be happy with their ill-gotten gains.
Let me seek only what is mine, what I have a right to,
   and let me learn to seek only what I need to fulfill
   my obligations and live decently in your sight.
Better to be poor and at peace.
Good night, Lord.

November 28

Flame of Love

"The one who doesn't love is among the living dead."
Lord, this is strangely reminiscent of the popular song,
   "What kind of fool am I, who never fell in love?"
Did today's songwriter take his cue from the Bible,
   or simply from the experience of the heart?
Life is worth living when you are in love,
   that is, when you live a life of love.
Your love for us, Lord, is an eternal flame;
   it burns without being exhausted,
   like the burning bush that Moses saw in the desert.
It warms our hearts, a symbol of your presence.
Grant that my love for you and others
   may burn as faithfully.
Good night, Lord.

Maturing

Young people look forward to independence,
    the maturing process we have all gone through.
As I pray this evening, I shudder
    at the imprudent, adolescent mistakes I have made.
Bless our young men and women
    with wisdom, patience, and prudence.
Let them not rush into what must take time:
    growing up to maturity in your sight, Lord.
Flying from the nest doesn't mean they're stunt pilots!
Help them, by your grace, to exercise self-control
    and to seek the counsel of others
    who have made that flight and made mistakes,
    and even made emergency landings.
Good night, Lord.

Unemployed

Lord, bless all who wish to earn their daily bread.
Many are off bright and early seeking employment.
For some, it is a new and exhilarating experience,
    finding a job after graduation.
For others, Lord, it is a matter of desperation
    because families are depending on them
    and "downsizing" companies have let them go.
They scan the classifieds and pursue interviews.
To be unemployed is almost to be without purpose.
Give them courage, incentive, and perseverance.
Quicken their creative powers.
Let them find supportive and satisfying occupations
    to benefit themselves, their families, and the world.
Good night, Lord.

December 1
Admitting Mistakes
Lord, some people never admit they are wrong.
There are times when apologies are in order;
    owning up, they feel, lessens them in others' eyes.
So they shield themselves with bravado,
    with whatever it takes not to appear imperfect.
The truth is an honest explanation
    builds the esteem of others.
People relate to candid behavior,
    when we are not engaged in transparent cover-ups.
When I am wrong, give me the courage and good sense
    to admit it to those I have wronged, and to you,
    whom my sin offends.
Good night, Lord.

December 2
Refreshment
What do I do, Lord, when concentrating is an effort,
    when I have to drag myself to my job,
    when it's so hard to get up in the morning,
    when I have no enthusiasm for any part of life,
    when I don't care, from one end of the day to the next?
How can I prime the pump?
I may need a good night's rest
    or a change in scenery,
    but you have assured me, Lord,
    that I can turn to you,
    my wellspring, my energy, my motivation:
    "Come to me, you who are weary
    and find life burdensome, and I will refresh you."
 Good night, Lord.

Close to God

Lord, a catchy line about the World Trade Center,
    those New York City skyscrapers, tells us:
    "This is the closest many of us will get to heaven."
I understand the ad about this colossal building,
    but I also happen to know, Lord,
    that I don't get closer to you
    the more I rise in the sky.
You are nearer to me than "up there" somewhere.
Heaven is my destiny, the goal of my life,
    but heaven is nothing if not you,
    and you are closer to me than I am to myself.
Make me conscious of your sacred indwelling,
    and let me abide forever in your presence.
Good night, Lord.

Quality of Life

Lord, there is much talk about the quality of life.
I wonder, what does that mean to people?
Is it the amount of material goods,
    comparing First World with the Third World?
Making daily life more pleasurable and comfortable
    in housing, diet, clothing, and cultural matters?
Vacations at resorts, dining out in chic restaurants?
Once, Lord, we sang a song that said
    the best things in life are free.
Quality of life comes from within, from the heart,
    from love and caring, from personal relationships,
    from commitment, forgiveness, and compassion.
Grant that I may have this kind of quality.
Good night, Lord.

December 5
Money Talks
Lord, I smile at the comment of the wealthy smart aleck
    on his deathbed: "If I can't take it with me, I won't go."
He went anyway.
Money: you can't take it with you,
    but you can't go anywhere without it.
Some build their careers around it,
    or select college courses based on it.
Others juggle the books, steal, or kill for it.
Help me to set genuine priorities,
    and to set limits on what I truly need.
How can I use it as a means to do your work,
    rather than as an end in itself, to serve only myself?
Inspire me to view money from your perspective.
Good night, Lord.

December 6
Good Shepherd
Have compassion, Lord, on those who find life empty.
They are like sheep without a shepherd.
Many do not know you or why you created them;
    they seem unaware of their origin and their destiny.
They are like sheep who lose their way,
    wandering into danger and confusion.
My prayer tonight, Lord, is that
    you touch them with your grace
    so that they may learn to know, love, and serve you.
From the beginning, you have made yourself known
    to those you love.
Continue to reach out to all of us who need you.
May we who know you share our good news.
Good night, Lord.

Holiness

Lord, I fear mistaken notions about being holy,
    such as appearing pious.
Holiness isn't found only in isolated piety.
It has to do with our relationship to you.
And that relationship is affected
    by our relationship to our brothers and sisters.
You have made it very clear, Lord,
    that whatever we do for one another,
    we do for you.
Holiness is fulfilling the two great commandments:
    to love you with all our hearts,
    and to love others as we love ourselves.
Give me the courage to strive to be holy.
Good night, Lord.

Fear

Fear is a monster that haunts all of us.
Lord, our fears are many and varied.
As I reflect during my evening prayer,
    it seems some folks fear even to reflect,
    lest skeletons—bad memories—rattle in their closets.
Walking down the street, they hesitate to say hello
    for fear of rejection.
People are timid about speaking to a group,
    or asking for donations, or asking if they can help.
Fear prevents them from doing good,
    or prompts them to do what they shouldn't.
With your grace, let those paralyzed by their feelings
    become free to show loving kindness to others.
Good night, Lord.

December 9

Suffering

When I'm suffering, shall I say, Lord,
    "Take this suffering from me; save me from this hour"?
Pain and distress are not unknown to you;
    you are not distant and disinterested, un-
    compassionate.
I'm sure you feel for us when we suffer.
As great as my suffering may be, Lord,
    I pray that when it comes, physical or emotional,
    I might accept it—even embrace it—
    to your great glory.
The lesson from holy Scripture makes sense.
Let my suffering render a special homage to you
    and send a special message to those who witness it.
Good night, Lord.

December 10

Honorable Thoughts

I pray you elevate the workings of my mind.
I know I can't always control what goes on there,
    but when I can, let my thoughts—
    about you, about others and myself—
    be, as St. Paul advises us,
    true, honorable, just, pure, loving, gracious.
We are encouraged to think good thoughts.
May my mind be, I ask you, Lord,
    a sanctuary of all that is good and noble
    and pleasing in your sight.
How good and spiritually uplifting it is
    to dwell on beneficial subjects
    and refuse admission to what is evil.
Good night, Lord.

Chief Value

I was thinking tonight, Lord, that I would like
    to develop the habit of pleasing you,
    of becoming a singleminded child of yours.
In this day of talking about values,
    let that be my chief inspiration.
Such values are deepened by reflection, prayer, effort.
Repeated good actions reflecting our values
    gives us an increased ease in doing what is right;
    they deepen our attitudes and resolutions even more.
The poet said, "I am the captain of my soul."
I can't say that unless you are with me, assisting me
    with your grace so that I may please you always.
May all my decisions be pleasing to you, Lord.
Good night, Lord.

Shortsighted Prayer

Some people pray, Lord, only when things go wrong.
  . . . like college students who write home
    only when they run out of money.
When tragedy strikes, when jobs are lost,
    when illness afflicts them,
    they find their way to church
    or get on their knees to pray.
Lord, how trying it must be for you.
Can't we turn to you just to say thanks,
    how good you are, or how sorry we are?
I pray, Lord, that I may speak with you on occasion
    and not feel I have to ask you for something.
Help me really to appreciate our personal relationship.
Good night, Lord.

December 13

Hiding One's Faith

Disguising my true feelings about you, Lord,
    will never do.
Or practicing my religion as a showpiece
    for all the world to see how holy I am—
    well, I know what you think of that!
If folks pretend to have a relationship with you
    and really don't, that's hypocritical.
But some seem to conceal their convictions and faith,
    as if they fear to offend or be subject to ridicule.
They avoid open, appropriate manifestations of faith.
Religion's a private matter, some trumpet.
How private?
No one should ever be ashamed to acknowledge you.
Good night, Lord.

December 14

Frame of Mind

This evening's prayer, Lord, is a time for me to declare
    that I do not ever want to take you for granted.
I want to keep trying to please you, to praise you,
    to speak with you and live in your presence.
The entertainer, the skilled laborer, the artist
    acquire the practiced art of control.
They make the difficult look easy, but this is possible
    only after long hours of practice and determination.
World leaders realize peace only with relentless,
    ongoing dialogue at the bargaining table.
Husbands and wives sustain their love
    by renewed daily devotion to each other's needs.
Grant that I may start each day in this frame of mind.
Good night, Lord.

Still in Love

Sometimes I meet spouses, Lord, who are still in love
    with each other after years of marriage.
Their love has grown deeper and stronger,
    in spite of occasional conflict and tension.
Theirs is a unique spiritual experience.
Is there a magical chemistry they bring to wedlock?
Are they on easy street
    now that they have been married a long time?
Bless them, Lord, as they continue their marriage.
Help them to learn new skills in communicating,
    in caring, in interpreting sensitivities and needs.
And may they never take their union for granted,
    but work at it each day of their lives together.
Good night, Lord.

First Moments

Once, not so long ago, Lord, there was a custom:
    new clothes were worn to church first.
It was a way to honor you.
People dedicated their days to you
    with the morning offering prayer.
The Scriptures tell of offering the first fruits
    of the harvest to you.
These customs helped us to dedicate our days,
    our possessions, our lives to you.
First moments were yours.
"Seek first the kingdom of God," you taught us.
I pray that you are always first in my life;
    all that I do and say and use I offer to you.
Good night, Lord.

December 17
Night Prayer

Is evening the right time for my prayer, Lord?
Bede, a monk from long, long ago, used to say
    that when the day's work is done
    and we are worn out by distractions,
    our minds are ready for this spiritual activity.
He saw an advantage at day's end,
    when the cares of the day were behind us
    and we could focus on you, Lord.
We are engrossed in responsibilities through the day
    and if we can pray then, turn to you a moment—
    let us be thankful for that.
But let us not allow you to be crowded out
    at this sacred time, night.
Good night, Lord.

December 18
Love

Lord, you told us that you are love
    and that it is to characterize our lives.
Help me, I pray, to learn deeply—in practice—
    what this means.
Love is upward-looking, keeping an eye on eternity.
It's what makes a person genuinely holy.
Love—not self-seeking—is outward-looking,
    wishing others well in every way.
It is single-minded, focusing on the welfare of others.
It is alert to their needs and to what is due to them.
Love is inward-looking, seeing you present
    and taking care of ourselves.
Teach me about love; teach me to love.
Good night, Lord.

Can't Live Without You

Sometimes, Lord, in romantic movies, the hero says
    to the heroine, "I can't live without you."
I want that to be my guiding thought all my days.
I don't mean that just for physical existence,
    that I depend upon you for every breath I take.
I mean more than that.
You are the center of my life, my reason for living
    and for dying.
You, Lord, are the Alpha and the Omega,
    the beginning and the end of my life.
You are all that matters.
Give me your grace to live that way.
How consoling it is to know you.
Good night, Lord.

Truth

I pray tonight, Lord, that I might always seek truth—
    wherever I may find it.
Truth is rooted in you and I have to be confident
    that if I find truth, I find you.
Truth stands on its own, independently,
    and I have to attempt to embrace it without prejudice.
Help me, Lord, as I struggle from my own point of view.
Loving you and seeking you,
    objectivity may be my biggest challenge.
My emotions must be under control;
    there can be no ulterior motives.
My journey of a lifetime, my pilgrimage,
    is a search for truth, for you.
Good night, Lord.

December 21

Memories

Memories are like old photographs, good for laughs,
    making us feel nostalgic for the way things were.
Like photos, Lord, they also fade with time.
How good it can be to page through albums
    to remember loved ones, recall good times with them.
"This is Uncle Sid, with Grandma and Grandpa
    at the circus . . . rest their souls."
"This is your mother—her First Communion picture;
    you look just like her," we remind the children.
Old photos remind us that we are different now;
    life is on the move and we have gotten older.
Thank you, Lord, for memories of loving people,
    and a fresh perspective enlightening the present.
Good night, Lord.

December 22

Stone Hearts

Lord, your Scriptures have told us that some people
    won't be convinced, or won't repent
    "even if one should rise from the dead."
You know how hard it can be to dissolve stone hearts.
This is easier said than done, isn't it, Lord?
Changing lifestyles, demanding sacrifice.
I know your grace can overcome anything.
What does it take to win over some people?
Threats? Promises of reward?
You are the Hound of Heaven,
    pursuing the sinner who flees you.
There is more than enough evidence of your love
    to melt hardened hearts.
Good night, Lord.

My Words

Nothing escapes you, Lord, not our thoughts
    and certainly not our words.
This is mysterious, marvelous, and awesome.
I praise you for it.
Before ever a word is on my tongue, you know it.
I can utter blessings and curses,
    gentle expressions and mean-spirited attacks.
Lord, let me use the power of speech in a loving way.
My mother used to tell me not to say anything at all
    if I couldn't say something good about someone.
Grant me the grace and good sense
    to speak lovingly to and about everyone.
May my every word praise you.
Good night, Lord.

Unbelievers

You, Lord, do not exist, to some people.
They don't know you;
    they don't think there's anything to know.
They see prayer and worship as a useless gesture.
What do you do with godless persons?
It has to be that you look with love
    on those who reject you, Lord,
    or at least doubt your existence.
You look into their hearts and see their sincerity.
You want us all to come to know you,
    despite our sins and hard-heartedness.
Your patience is great,
    but you compel no one against their will.
Good night, Lord.

Ecumenism

Ecumenism means "worldwide,"
   and that's the size of the challenge for religious unity.
People pray to you on all continents, Lord,
   just as I am this evening.
Do you smile at our varied images of you?
At the different ways we approach you?
At the discussions, or arguments, we have about you?
We are opposed on some basic beliefs
   and even on some moral issues.
If we are not to compromise our principles,
   help us to appreciate where we are united.
This must be a priority in our prayer.
Bless the sincere at heart.
Good night, Lord.

December 26

Environment

This is your world, Lord, and we are responsible for it.
We must struggle to keep our air breathable,
   our water drinkable, and our soil plantable.
This fragile planet is our sacred trust.
Let us not live here as if it is for humans alone,
   and only for a few centuries or so.
Even Isaiah, your prophet, spoke about ecology,
   telling us you didn't create the world to be a waste.
We are all connected, Lord, to you and to one another.
Inspire us to keep creation beautiful and livable.
It's not that we have inherited it from our ancestors;
   we have borrowed it from our grandchildren.
Grant us the wisdom to keep it intact for them.
Good night, Lord.

Information Age

Lord, it's a highly intensified, sophisticated world
   with computers, radio, television, lasers, and press,
   but we can't live by information alone.
Our basic human longings—
   for personal relationships, for example—
   need more than that.
Our hearts are restless, Lord.
Internet and the info age can't satisfy the hungry heart.
Our longing for you isn't content
   with a computer printout or a fax message.
Help us to use these technological blessings
   to run society smoothly, to form community,
   so that they may ultimately lead us to you.
Good night, Lord.

Ridicule

It's hard to be good, Lord, when people deride us.
Their laughter and sneers can be compelling weapons.
Such pressure can make us appear foolish.
Let the psalmist's attitude be mine:
"Though the proud may deride me, Lord,
   I will keep to your law."
Help me to persevere, despite the ridicule.
There is not a saint in history
   who was exempt from this challenge.
There's the test: doing your will
   even though we will be mocked for it.
I pray that I may have this courage:
   to appear foolish for your name's sake.
Good night, Lord.

December 29

Beauty

I thank you, Lord, for all the beauty in the world,
    the beauty we see as well as the beauty we don't;
    it is all a reflection of you.
Help me to appreciate more and more
    what is truly beautiful around me,
    and to promote beauty in whatever way I can:
    by supporting the arts,
    by creating what is beautiful myself,
    by encouraging care for the environment.
But external beauty is not everything.
Let me also value internal beauty:
    moral courage, the kind thought,
    the giving personality, the struggle through adversity.
Good night, Lord.

December 30

Prepared

Strange, Lord, to be thinking about the fable
    about the grasshopper and ant during evening prayer.
The ant works hard, storing food for the winter,
    while the grasshopper plays all day,
    dancing the summer away.
When the snow falls, the ant has provisions,
    but the grasshopper is out in the cold, hungry,
    because he didn't anticipate the challenge
    and was too lazy to work at the preparations.
The point for my life is clear, Lord.
Give me the grace to be prepared,
    to live with my eyes wide open
    for the day I must give an account of my life.
Good night, Lord.

Eloquence

Some people, Lord, have a way with words;
    they say things appropriately, beautifully,
    sensitively, imaginatively, movingly.
The pride of their language mentors,
    they work diligently at their compositions.
When there is great passion,
    some are more than eloquent, even poetic.
How wonderful to communicate artfully
    and to speak the truth at the same time.
Thank you, Lord, for this gift—
    for whomever you have given it to.
May their best words, in verse or prose,
    be for your honor and glory.
Good night, Lord.

Of Related Interest...

Good Morning, Lord
Everyday Prayers for Everyday People
Joseph T. Sullivan
Here are 366 brief, yet thoughtful prayers, one for each day of the year. They deal with ordinary events and feelings, as well as those arising from extraordinary situations.
0-89622-593-3, 200 pp, $9.95

A New Look at Prayer
Searching for Bliss
William Huebsch
Readers will find a guide for listening to God, for discerning and discovering who they are and who they can be.
0-89622-458-9, 136 pp, $7.95
Audiobook: Two 60-minute cassettes, $16.95
Audiobook: Two 45-minute cassettes, $16.95

Psalms for Times of Trouble
John Carmody
Carmody is openly realistic in this book of prayers forged in the darkness and trouble of his own battle with terminal cancer. Yet throughout there is a hope of the eternal kindness and mercy of God.
0-89622-614-X, 168 pp, $9.95

Who We Are Is How We Pray
Charles Keating
Draws on the 16 personality types identified in the Myers-Briggs personality profile and matches each to a suitable form and style of spirituality.
0-89622-321-3, 168 pp, $7.95

Available at religious bookstores or from:

 **TWENTY-THIRD PUBLICATIONS**
P.O. Box 180 • Mystic, CT 06355

To order or request a free catalog of other quality books and video call:
1-800-321-0411